940.53 TES

LANCASHIRE COUNTY LIBRARY

This book must be returned on or before the date marked below

11 APR 1969

MONTHLY LOAN

28. MAY 1969

-5. SEP 1969

23. AUG. 1969

20. FEB 1970

11. MAR
-3. APR 1970

18 MAR 1970

MAWSON

-4. DEC. 1970

Flynn
9/11/10

17. NOV. 1970

26. MAY 1971

14. JAN. 1972

ML

-4. JAN. 1972

-6. OCT. 1972

RS

WITHDRAWN FROM
LANCASHIRE LIBRARIES

Lancashire County Library

30118092781065

Please tell the Librarian if you
COUNTY LIBRARY, PRESTON.

D1582445

THE TESTAMENT OF ADOLF HITLER

(February–April 1945)

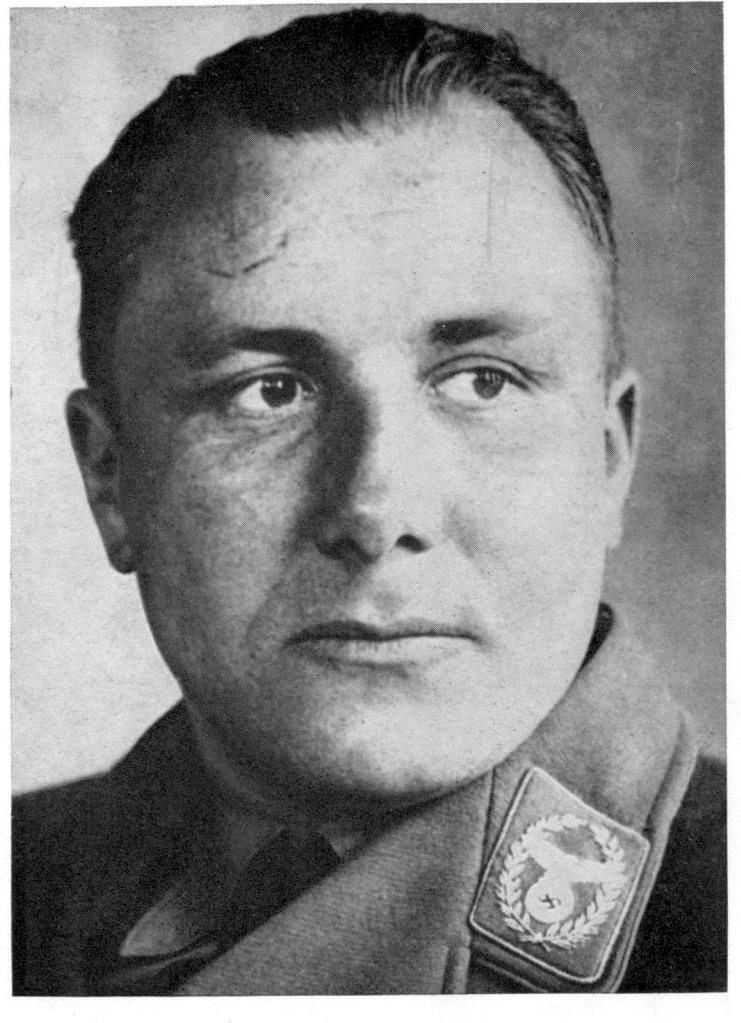

Martin Bormann, 1941

THE TESTAMENT
OF ADOLF HITLER

The Hitler-Bormann Documents
February – April 1945
edited by François Genoud

Translated from the German
by Colonel R. H. Stevens

With an Introduction by
H. R. Trevor-Roper
Professor of Modern History
in the University of Oxford

CASSELL · LONDON

CASSELL & COMPANY LTD

35 Red Lion Square · London WC1
and at
MELBOURNE · SYDNEY · TORONTO · CAPE TOWN · AUCKLAND

―――――――

First published in France under the title
Le Testament Politique de Hitler
by Librairie Arthème Fayard, 1959

ⓒ Librairie Arthème Fayard 1959

This English translation ⓒ François Genoud 1960
First published in book form in Great Britain 1961

Set in 11-13 *Plantin and printed
in Great Britain by*

THE SHENVAL PRESS, LONDON, HERTFORD AND HARLOW

F.1160

CONTENTS

INTRODUCTION

BY

PROFESSOR H. R. TREVOR-ROPER

A new document has recently been discovered, concerning Adolf Hitler. It is a document of great historical interest: Hitler's political testament, his last general reflections on the war which by now he had lost, the last window to be opened into that dark chamber, so noisome, hideous and haunted and yet so charged with real if terrible explosive force, his mind.

What a mind Hitler had! Surely we cannot deny that. It is easy to be disgusted by it. It was vulgar and violent, coarse, cruel and horrible, filled with festering litter and old lumber from his rancorous, seedy past; and yet it was also—if we can see past this obvious and odious furniture—a mind of extraordinary power: it could clarify as well as simplify, illustrate as well as distort, make the future as well as deform the past. To deny Hitler's mental power, to say (as some say) that he was mere froth casually thrown up by the swirling waters of social change, seems to me a desperate gesture. Even if we do not accept Hitler's own estimate of himself as a unique historical phenome-

I

non, a phoenix in human history, born to transform, alone in a single lifetime, the history of the world, we must yet admit that he did what no other man in our history has done. He devised, made and carried out a great revolution from start to finish, from nothing to world empire. Other great revolutions have regularly devoured their children. Hitler alone was always a devourer, never devoured. He was the Rousseau, the Mirabeau, the Robespierre, the Napoleon of his revolution: its Marx, its Lenin, its Trotzky, its Stalin. In character and mentality he may have been far inferior to most of these men, but at least he did what none of them did: he controlled his revolution through all its stages, even in defeat. This alone argues a remarkable understanding of the forces with which he conjured. He may have been a hideous historical phenomenon, but at least he was an important historical phenomenon, and we cannot afford to pass him by.

Three times in the history of the Nazi revolution windows have now been opened through his *Table Talk* into the recesses of Hitler's mind, and this new document is the third of them. Each window has been opened, as if on purpose, at a crucial period in that history. The first was in 1932-3, in the days of the *Machtübernahme*, the seizure of power in Germany. In those days Hitler, elated with the prospect of seizing and exercising power—power which, once seized, he was resolved never to give up—spoke at large to his 'inner circle' of political associates about the aims and methods of his rule. At that time conservatives, both in Germany and abroad, fondly thought of Hitler as one of themselves: a dictator of course, but a dictator of the Right. In his intimate conversations Hitler now revealed, although only to his intimate associates, the falsity of such an idea. In terrifying detail he described the wholesale revolution which he planned to unleash in the world, the dark forces of destruction which he intended to yoke to the chariot of his power. Of these conversations, as far as we know, there is no official record. But there is an unofficial record. One of Hitler's intimate circle, Hermann Rauschning, was really a conservative, and when he heard this radical programme so powerfully and so convincingly set forth, he was appalled. He separated himself from 'the Revolution of Destruction' and in 1939 published his record of *Hitler's Table Talk*. Unfortunately, though no one now doubts its authenticity this record was not then believed. Such a programme, men said, was inconceivable. Rauschning must have invented it. I am told that Neville Chamberlain, who was convinced that he really understood Hitler, declared roundly of Rauschning's record that he did not believe a word of it—just as men had refused to believe a word of Hitler's openly declared programme in *Mein Kampf*.

Eight years after the *Machtübernahme* another window was opened into Hitler's mind. In 1941 Hitler had carried out, almost to the letter, the programme described to Rauschning. Then he had been on the eve of the conquest of power in Germany; now he was on the eve of an even greater conquest: the conquest of world-empire. For by 1941 all resistance to Hitler in Europe had been broken. The verdict of 1918 had been reversed. From the North Cape to Crete, from Danzig to the Pyrenees, his armies were everywhere victorious, and all the forces of Europe united at last under invincible, revolutionary German leadership were about to be hurled, and were being hurled, against the one remaining Continental power which Hitler respected: Communist Russia, whose vast area was now to be converted into the colonial *Lebensraum* of united, industrial, German Europe. No wonder Hitler was elated as he felt the first crunch of victory in the east, as his victorious armies swept forward, on all fronts, to Leningrad, Moscow and Kiev. It was in these circumstances that he decided once again to give posterity a piece of his mind. Only this time there was to be an official, not an unofficial record. Posterity was not to rely on the indiscretions of another Rauschning, but on an authentic, approved, official transcript.

The arrangements were made, as was natural, by Hitler's obedient secretary Martin Bormann, the faithful, prosaic, indefatigable, and himself thoroughly unoriginal high-priest of Hitler's new revelation. To Hitler's headquarters, in East Prussia or in the Ukraine, where he held forth every day to bewildered generals, politicians and secretaries, Bormann summoned successive officials who sat unobtrusively in corners taking down the copious Holy Writ—Hitler's conversations, or rather monologues, on the power he had achieved and the empire he was to conquer and create. When the officials had recorded the gospel Bormann himself read it carefully through, annotated and corrected it, and sent it to be preserved for posterity in the Party Archives, until the time should come for official publication. In fact, as in the case of

Rauschning's record, the publication was unofficial after all. Bormann's records—the *Bormann-Vermerke* as they were called—were discovered after the war and published in France in 1952 as *Libres Propos sur la Guerre et la Paix*, by Adolf Hitler, in England in 1953 as *Hitler's Table Talk*.

As far as Hitler's plans went, it is probable that the *Table Talk* of 1941–2 was intended as his last political testament. It was a full account of his plans for the final achievement of Nazism, the setting up of the Thousand-Year Reich. When that was done what was there left to plan? Beyond world-conquest where can even a world-conqueror go? But alas the world is full of disappointments, especially for world-conquerors, who often find, when they can go no further forward, that they are obliged to go back. Three years afterwards, at the beginning of 1945, Hitler found himself face to face with a new prospect. Something had gone wrong since 1942. In the east the Russians had resisted; in the west, the British had survived, the Americans had come in; in the south, Italy had collapsed; and now, from east and west and south, the armies of the great alliance which Hitler had aroused against him were closing remorselessly in. In vain Hitler had struck back on all fronts: the Gothic line in Italy was broken, the Ardennes offensive in the west had failed, Himmler's new 'Army Group Vistula' in the east was a fiasco. By the beginning of February 1945 it was no longer possible, even for Hitler, to believe in a German victory. Nothing now seemed able to stop the gradual closure upon Germany of the great armies which, at last, were being carried forward by the consciousness of strength, the taste of victory, the passion of the world's revenge.

What was Hitler to do in February 1945 when all his dreams, once so nearly realized, seemed about to crumble? Of course he would not admit that they were crumbling. Victory, he insisted, was still possible; if only one held out, even against impossible odds, Providence might yet intervene. After all it had intervened for Frederick the Great. In 1762 he too had been cooped up in Berlin, surrounded by remorselessly closing allied armies. He had even decided, in despair, to take his own life. And yet, at the last moment, his heroism had been rewarded. Providence had intervened. The Tsarina of Russia had died. There had been a diplomatic revolution. He was saved. Even so today might not heroism, will-power, obstinacy be rewarded? 'Like the great Frederick, we too are combating against a coalition, and a coalition, remember, is not a stable entity; it exists only by the will of a handful of men. If Churchill were suddenly to disappear, everything could change in a flash. . . . '

So Hitler reasoned; and yet he could not entirely persuade himself. Providence might intervene—he hoped against hope that it would; and yet it might not. And if not, what then? In the practical world there was, Hitler always insisted, only one thing to do. Like Frederick the Great, he would wait till the last minute and then, unless a miracle happened, take his own life. But meanwhile, in the intellectual world, there was also something to do. Hitler's last political testament, the testament of 1941–2 which presupposed the beginning of the Thousand-Year

6

Reich, was obviously now somewhat out of date. It was necessary, for the sake of intellectual tidiness, and to ensure that one had the last word, to issue a postscript. So once again Hitler prepared to open a window into his mind. Even now, in the hour of defeat and under the pressure of events, though broken in health, a shadow of his former self, pale and stooping, with glazed eyes and trembling, half-paralysed limbs, he prepared to issue his final chapter of the Holy Writ: a stop-press, last-minute extra instalment of his *Table Talk*.

Once again the arrangements were made by Bormann. Bormann and Goebbels were by now the only disciples whom Hitler trusted, and Bormann, even more than Goebbels, was constantly at Hitler's side. Besides, Bormann was, in one sense, a better interpreter than Goebbels: he had no ideas of his own with which to distort, however unwittingly, his master's voice. And this time it was really Bormann who handled everything: there were no officials in unobtrusive corners—indeed there were no unobtrusive corners in that cramped, underground Bunker beneath the Chancellery in Berlin. So Bormann himself took charge of every detail: his own large, loose, formless signature is there, authenticating the typewritten pages of these new *Bormann-Vermerke* which were compiled all through February 1945. At the end of February Hitler had completed his work: only once thereafter—on 2nd April—did he add a last postscript. Then the documents were put away, in Bormann's care, while Hitler and his diminished circle waited, hoping against hope for the Tsarina to die.

Oh that Tsarina! What an obsession she became in those last days of waiting, when only chance and death seemed to offer hope to the besieged dwellers in the Berlin Bunker! Once indeed their patience seemed rewarded, the miracle seemed to have happened. While Bormann patiently recorded Hitler's utterances, Goebbels, the impresario of the Nazi movement, was preparing the final *mise-en-scène*. Already, in March, he had set the stage for 'a real Twilight-of-the-Gods scene'. Now in April, soon after Hitler's last oracular 'conversation', Goebbels had sought to soothe the Führer by reading aloud, yet again, that chapter of Carlyle's *History of Frederick the Great* in which Frederick had been saved from suicide and defeat by the last-minute death of the Tsarina. A few days later they were still talking about the Tsarina when an electric thrill shot from the Propaganda Ministry to the Bunker. Pale with excitement, Goebbels rushed to the telephone. 'My Führer,' he exclaimed, 'I congratulate you. Fate has laid low your greatest enemy . . . it is the miracle of the House of Brandenburg: the Tsarina is dead!' The Tsarina was not Churchill but Roosevelt who had died on the eve of victory, on 12th April 1945.

Unfortunately, though the Tsarina died, this time there was no diplomatic revolution. Once again gloom descended on the Bunker, and by 17th April hope had begun its last ebb. On that day a Nazi official then attending Hitler in Berlin was ordered by him to leave the city. He was to go to Bad Gastein and arrange for the removal of the German gold reserves to a salt-mine in Thuringia. Before he left, Hitler told him that Bormann would entrust him with certain documents which he was to convey to distant safety. Bormann duly gave him a sealed package. This package was the last *Bormann-Vermerke*, Hitler's last *Table Talk*, the documents which have now come to light. They were sent to be preserved, together with the older record of 1941–2, in the Party Archives. Five days later, on 22nd April, Hitler authorized a general exodus from the Chancellery: the ring was closing, and all who wished to go were allowed to escape from beleaguered Berlin. By the next day the ring was in fact closed: the final siege had begun, and from now on no other documents that we know were sent out of the Bunker, save only Hitler's last will and testament and the certificate of his last-minute marriage to Eva Braun. By 30th April Hitler had taken the practical as well as the intellectual steps which history, defeat and the example of Frederick the Great had imposed upon him. Even the Tsarina's death, this time, had not saved him: Providence had not intervened; so he took his own life.

Meanwhile, what of the documents? By the time of Hitler's death the bearer had already deposited them, still sealed, in a safe place—in the vaults of a bank in Bad Gastein. Soon afterwards the bearer was himself arrested, charged with various war crimes and condemned to a term of imprisonment. While serving his sentence, he was constantly afraid that the documents in Bad Gastein would be revealed and that their revelation would incriminate him still further in the eyes of the victors. He wished they could be destroyed. And finally he found an opportunity of destroying them. Even from his prison he found it possible, sometimes, to communicate with the outer world, and so he sent a message to a trusted legal friend authorizing him to go to Bad Gastein and claim from their custodian the documents he had deposited. After extracting some personal papers, he was to burn the rest. 'The rest' was Hitler's last *Table Talk*.

The legal friend did as he was told. He claimed the documents, extracted the personal papers, and prepared to burn the rest. But before burning them he looked to see what they were and saw that they were historic documents, of interest to posterity. What was he to do? On the one hand his client had clearly told him to burn them, and therefore it was his private duty to do so. On the other hand the Voice of History commanded him with equal clarity to preserve them: therefore it was his public duty to do this. In this dilemma the lawyer devised a neat, lawyerly compromise. First, he had a photostatic copy of the documents made, and preserved this copy in secrecy. Thus he discharged his duty to posterity. Then he solemnly destroyed the original documents, and thus discharged his duty to his client. Of course, the neat, lawyerly compromise could not last for ever, and in fact, some years later, the original bearer of the documents, on emerging from prison, had to be told the truth. He was not at all pleased. But in the end he too compromised with historic necessity. He agreed to condone the *fait accompli*, provided that his own part in the affair was wrapped in convenient ambiguity. So the documents were once again reprieved and became available for publication.

Such is the background of these new documents which

chance has now revealed in Germany. Of their authenticity there can be no doubt: their history, their content and Bormann's own familiar signature attest it at every point. To anyone who has studied Hitler's mind, the internal evidence alone would be conclusive. These documents are, in a sense, Hitler's full political testament, to which his official 'political testament', signed on 29th April, together with his private will (which appointed Bormann as his executor), is merely a brief, formal tailpiece. For in these monologues, uttered in the hour of evident defeat from which only a miracle could save him, Hitler ranged over all the problems of the war which he had both won and lost. Hitler's first recorded *Table Talk*, the talk recorded by Rauschning, uttered in the exciting days of the *Machtübernahme*, could be sub-titled, 'What I shall do with my power in Germany'. His second recorded *Table Talk*, the already published *Bormann-Vermerke*, uttered in the exciting days of world-conquest, could be sub-titled, 'What I shall do with the conquered world'. This third recorded *Table Talk*, uttered in the last days of failure and defeat, when world-conquest and power in Germany had both dissolved before his eyes, could be sub-titled, 'Why did I not win? What went wrong?'

And what did go wrong? Did Hitler's error consist in making war, or in making this or that war? In fighting Russia while Britain was still undefeated? In turning against Russia, which was so hard to conquer, when he could so easily have mopped up the Mediterranean, North Africa, the Levant? In not taking Gibraltar in 1940? Or

was it simply a matter of timing? Should he have postponed his world war till 1942 (as he had thought in 1938),
or unleashed it in 1938 (as he thought in 1945)? Was he
wrong in his relations with Britain, or with Spain? Was he
too lenient to France, or too indulgent to that great man,
'my equal, perhaps even—in some respects—my superior',
Mussolini, who, however, was saddled with the Italian, as
he with the German people? Should he have been more
conservative, an ally of those 'arrogant islanders', the
British, or more radical: should he have put himself at the
head of revolutionary, anti-colonial, proletarian move-
ments throughout the world, even if that meant bursting
the framework of society and his alliance with Italy,
France, Spain, those worthless Latin allies, the source of
half his woes?

All these were possibilities. All of them had to be considered in this last great *post-mortem* on the war and its
disastrous outcome. And Hitler is thinking of them, thinking aloud. Again and again his mind settles on those crucial
turning-points in which, as it now seems, a wrong turning
may have been taken. Most men who have failed in their
ambitions indulge in such retrospective thinking. Their
conclusions, however, cannot always be trusted. They
think of the steps which they might have taken, but often
they forget the fatal obstacles which might have prevented
those steps, the effective counter-measures which might
have frustrated them. And then the human memory is a
faulty organ which tends, by selection, to favour its owner.
Hitler's memory was particularly good at this favourable
selection. Look, for instance, at his memories of 1940,

and particularly of his attempt to bring General Franco into the war on his side.

'I have sometimes asked myself,' Hitler observed casually in 1945, 'whether we were not wrong, in 1940, not to have drawn Spain into the war. It would have been too easy for words to do so, for Spain was burning to follow Italy's example and become a member of the victor's club. . . . However, since Spain had really nothing tangible to contribute, I came to the conclusion that her direct intervention was not desirable.' Even without Spanish intervention, he added, it would have been easy to occupy Gibraltar with commandos, without any declaration of war but with Franco's connivance. The only difficulty would have been not to bring Franco in but to keep him out—'particularly as we had failed, a few weeks previously, to prevent Italy from flying to the rescue of our victory'.

'The easiest thing in the world' . . . 'with Franco's connivance'. . . . Who would suspect, from these condescending phrases, the real facts about Hitler's courtship of Franco in 1940? How Hitler begged Franco to enter the war, or at least to admit the German army, only to be constantly refused; how Hitler had condescended to go in person to the Pyrenees to woo that obstinate dictator, only to be kept arguing for nine hours and, in the end, sent empty away; how he had then declared to Mussolini that he would rather have three or four teeth out than go through such an interview again, and had begged the Duce to take over the conversations and win over the 'prodigal son' of the Axis; and how even the Duce had failed to move the cold, factual, hard-bargaining Caudillo. So bitter was Hitler about Franco's refusal that for two years afterwards the mere mention of his name would bring a rush of blood to his head, and of words to his lips. Franco was 'cowardly and irresolute', an 'inflated peacock' smugly seated 'on his pretender's throne'; but for his 'idiotic' behaviour Gibraltar would have been won in five days and the British and Americans could never have landed in North Africa and pierced open the 'soft under-belly of the Axis'. Then for another two years a taboo had fallen on the very name of Franco; it might not even be mentioned in the Führer's hearing. And yet now in 1945 we find Hitler saying in this calm, casual manner, that it would have been 'too easy for words' to have brought Spain into the war in 1940—in fact it was almost impossible to prevent it! How much Hitler had conveniently forgotten of the events of 1940!

In Hitler's *post-mortem* of the war there are many such errors and omissions. And yet does it matter? If we read Hitler's table talk it is not in search of facts, but rather in search of light upon his mind and character. We do not want to know why Hitler lost the war, but why he thought he lost the war—which of course may be a very different matter. On this question the newly discovered table talk gives remarkably clear answers: answers that are interesting not only for the amount of truth that they may contain, but also for the light which they shed on the aims and character both of Hitler himself and of National Socialism.

First of all, let us consider the errors to which Hitler does not admit. Some might say that Hitler erred in unleashing a world war. To that Hitler never agrees. It was not he who made war, he insists: it was the Allies, and they made it not merely in 1939 but in 1933, by refusing to surrender in advance to every demand made in the name of 'the fundamental rights of the German people'. For National Socialism, he insists, had an inherent, pre-scriptive right to conquer the world and any opposition, any lack of sympathy, automatically justified it in taking by force whatever was not freely granted. Moreover, Hitler added, the West never had any right to resist him because he was really—if only people would understand—fighting for the West. Europe, he declared, must be united, in order to resist Russia: and he, and he alone, knew how to unite it, under a German tyranny which would 'dis-infect the West', 'lance the Communist abscess', 'get rid of the Jewish poison'; therefore it was the duty of the West to help, not to hinder, his work. Hindrance was criminal, lunatic, suicidal: an attack by a drowning man on his saviour, who of course, in such circumstances, was entitled to knock him on the head. 'I have been Europe's last hope. She proved incapable of refashioning herself by means of voluntary reform. She showed herself imper-vious to charm and persuasion. To take her, I had to use violence.' It was bitter necessity, Hitler always insists, which compelled him to attack Europe—so different from the wilful malevolence with which Europe resisted him.

If Hitler did not admit error in making war on Europe, what about his attack on Russia? Many Germans believed that this was his fatal error. If only Hitler had been con-tent with his gains, they said . . . if only he had stopped after the conquest of France . . . he would then have made Germany undisputed master of Europe, reversed the verdict of 1918, restored the Bismarckian Reich, and done all this at trivial cost. He would have won a real blitzkrieg and created for German arms a reputation which none would have dared to challenge. Even Britain would have had to come to terms ultimately with the new reality. Surely a deal could have been arranged in the end with that other Nordic power which the Germans, even Hitler himself, secretly respected and only hated because, like some self-assured effortless aristocrat, it declined to return that respect.

Sometimes in his retrospective moments Hitler seems to admit this possibility. If only Britain had been sensible in 1940 or 1941, he would exclaim, what an idyllic peace would have been established between two proud, Nordic powers, each victorious over a feeble Latin enemy, Germany over France, England over Italy! England could then have concentrated on her empire, which Germany would generously have guaranteed, and Germany would have settled down to digest Europe, to enjoy victory, to liquidate the Jews. Surely Britain—the real Britain, not Jew-ridden adventurers like Churchill—would understand and sympathize with such moderate, reasonable ambitions.

So Hitler would say; but when we look further we always discover that his ambition was not really so simple as that. Peace with Britain in 1940 would not have been the end of his war: it would have been the beginning. Its purpose would not have been settlement but redirection:

'Germany, secure in her rear, could then have thrown herself, heart and soul, into her real task, the mission of my life, the *raison d'être* of National Socialism—the destruction of Bolshevism'. 'It is eastwards, only and always eastwards, that the veins of our life must expand.' To have evaded war with Russia might have made sense for the old, monarchist Germany of 1914 or for those conservatives who now sought to revive that old Germany, but to the new, revolutionary, Nazi Germany such an evasion was unthinkable. The war with Russia was not a diversion which, if unsuccessful, would be an error: it was the be-all and end-all of Nazism. Failure in it might be final disaster; but to leave it unattempted would be to betray the mission of Germany.

When we realize this we realize Hitler's attitude towards Britain. In his eyes the real crime of Britain was not merely our refusal to be beaten by Germany: it was our insistence on continuing to fight even while he was engaged with Russia. But for British resistance, he maintained, he would have conquered Russia. Hence his paroxysms of hatred were not directed against Russia, the victim who struck back, but against those incorrigible islanders whom he had wooed in vain and who had now robbed him of his conquest, his final solution. 'Always it has been this Britain who barred Europe's way to prosperity. But now', he added with wishful spite, 'she is aged and enfeebled, though not less vicious and evil'; and he looked forward to the gradual extinction of that Jew-rotted race which, he hoped, would die of hunger and tuberculosis in their accursed island.

If Hitler thought he had been right to make war, and right to invade Russia, in spite of Britain, where did he go wrong? Had he perhaps launched his war too soon? No, he would not admit that. Russia had to be attacked: a dozen reasons demanded haste. Time, population, everything favoured the Russians if he were to delay. In fact, exclaimed Hitler, it would have been far better if he had launched his war first against the West to unite it, then against Russia to conquer it, in 1938, instead of in 1939. It was then, he thought (in retrospect), that his military readiness had been greatest, his excuses most plausible. But alas, in *morale* Germany had not yet been ready: it was still encumbered with reactionary generals and diplomats. And then there was the infamous behaviour of the Machiavellian Chamberlain who, at Munich, surrendered to all Hitler's demands and thus deprived him of a good excuse for making war. Of course, Hitler insists, we should have struck at once in 1938. 'But they gave way on every point. The cowards! they yielded to all our demands. In such circumstances it was very difficult to take the initiative and launch a war.' To Hitler, in retrospect, Munich—his greatest bloodless triumph—was a disaster. He would have preferred a bloody triumph. 'However, you can hardly blame me if the British and French accepted at Munich every demand I made of them!'

Where then *could* Hitler blame himself? Was there *any* crucial misfortune which might have been avoided if only he had decided or acted differently? As he ranged over the history of the war, Hitler admitted many errors of detail, many misjudgments of character—always adding that his

18

errors had of course been on the side of generosity. He was such a gentleman, he could not believe that other people could be such cads. Still, these errors were not fatal: it was not they which had ruined his plans, turning the universal victory of 1941 into the universal defeat of 1945. Then at last, having excluded all other possibilities, he pinpointed the real cause of disaster. In itself it was a technical error, a mere matter of date; but it made all the difference to the result; and it sprang in turn from a major error of judgment by himself, an error which he admitted and which provoked him to a whole new expression of his philosophy.

The technical error was simple. Hitler launched his war against Russia on 21st June 1941. It was intended as a blitzkrieg, to be over in one summer. And it very nearly was. And if it had been, think of the result! The victory in the east—the be-all and end-all of Nazism—would have been achieved before Britain was able to attack in the west, before America had come in. What then could Britain have done? What indeed except recognize the facts, sooner or later, and surrender? And yet instead of this, by the narrowest of margins, Hitler had been stopped by the Russian winter. In his race against the season he had been defeated by a few weeks. With only a few more weeks of campaigning weather in 1941, he would have been victorious over all enemies four years ago. . . . No wonder he was mortified when he looked back over the last four years of mounting disaster ending, now, in total ruin! And the maddening thing was that his plans had allowed him another five weeks. The invasion of Russia had been planned not for 21st June, but for the 15th May. Why then had he allowed that fatal postponement?

The answer is simple. He was let down by Mussolini. For already by October 1940 Mussolini was smarting under the double sense of Hitler's victories and his own humiliations. In spite of all his own past services, for which Hitler declared himself so grateful ('Mussolini, I will never forget', he had wired in 1938), the Duce now found himself ordered about, unheeded, almost insulted. Hitler took huge decisions without even informing him; or if he did inform him it was by summoning him to the telephone, or sending the German ambassador to wake him at the most inconvenient hours. 'I am sick and tired of being rung for', Mussolini would complain to his son-in-law Ciano. And then one day he could bear it no longer. He resolved to show his independence. 'Hitler always faces me with a *fait accompli*', he told Ciano on 12th October 1940. 'This time I am going to pay him back in his own coin. He will find out from the newspapers that I have occupied Greece. In this way the balance will be restored.'

Poor Mussolini! His Greek adventure was a total disaster. It led to the Yugoslav revolt, the British expedition, and in the end he had to be rescued by Hitler. Hitler did rescue him (though he also, in Mussolini's phrase, 'fairly smacked my fingers'); but in doing so he completely upset his own time-table. On 15th May he was not yet ready to invade Russia. Because of Mussolini the invasion of Russia was put off till 21st June. And because of that postponement the victory, which seemed so certain, was still not quite won when the terrible, premature Russian winter came. It had escaped, narrowly indeed, but for ever.

This then was to Hitler the fatal turning-point of the war: those lost five weeks which could have been saved if only Mussolini had not been his ally in war. And that, of course, was his error. Why, oh why, he asked, had he ever relied on those fickle Latins? They had brought him nothing but disaster. In the 1930s, at great cost, he had installed a Latin dictator in Spain, hoping for an ally, only to be deceived by that miserable clerical renegade, General Franco. In France he had shown himself merciful—had only occupied half of it—only to be deceived by that miserable old reactionary Marshal Pétain. What, he exclaimed, had caused him to forget his own prophetic insight of long ago—when he had written in *Mein Kampf* that 'France must be annihilated'? And now Italy too had ruined him. To the Duce, of course, in spite of all his faults, he was still bound by ancient admiration, genuine affection, everlasting gratitude. And yet how disastrous Italy's belligerency had been! Hitler almost wept to think of it. That 'idiotic campaign in Greece!' 'If the war had remained a war conducted by Germany, and not by the Axis, we should have been in a position to attack Russia by 15th May 1941. Doubly fortified by the fact that our forces had known nothing but decisive and irrefutable victory, we should have been able to conclude the campaign before winter came. How differently everything has turned out!'

But when Hitler considered the fatal error of his trust

in the Latin peoples, and especially in Italy, he did not stop here. Italy to him had not only proved a feeble ally, a military liability, a 'soft underbelly' through which the heart of the Axis had been pierced. There were also further consequences. Italy was a colonial power with an empire in Africa in which the Duce, unfortunately, made himself ridiculous by imperial postures. As a revolutionary dictator Hitler despised these archaic postures, but as a loyal ally he felt obliged to support them. Moreover, in the adjoining French colonies, he had also to support French imperialism—for empires hang together and revolt is contagious. Besides, Italy claimed the French inheritance, and claimed it intact. The necessity of the Italian alliance committed Hitler to support of imperialism in Africa. And yet, in retrospect, he reflected, how unfortunate that support had been!

For as the war went on and the old Europe proved its toughness, Hitler's genuine social radicalism had become more open, more intense. He wished he had supported the Spanish Communists—who were not of course real Communists—instead of Franco, the dukes and the Church. The German aristocracy, he now saw, were his enemies at home: the 20th July 1944 had shown that. Why, he asked himself, had he not been more radical altogether? Why had he not pursued a revolutionary policy everywhere—in Germany, in Europe, in Africa? What interest had Germany in colonies beyond the sea? In *Mein Kampf* he had disowned them, and he had been consistent ever since. Germany had now no such colonies to lose, and none to gain. Therefore why had he not thumped the

THE TESTAMENT

I

Pitt and Churchill—Pitt paves the way for Empire,
Churchill digs its grave—Europe has lost her supremacy
—Great Britain ought to have accepted a negotiated
Peace—The Third Reich was forced into war—Misfor-
tune and adversity, the parents of great resurrections

4th February 1945

Churchill seems to regard himself as a second Pitt. What a
hope! In 1793, Pitt was thirty-four years old. Churchill unfortunately is an old man, capable, and only just capable
at that, of carrying out the orders of that madman,
Roosevelt.

In any case, the situations are in no way comparable.
Take your mind back for a moment to the conditions in
Pitt's time. From England's point of view, he was per-
fectly right in refusing to have any truck with Napoleon.
By maintaining, as he did, a firm attitude under impos-
sible conditions, he was safeguarding for his country such

chance as it had of playing the role which subsequently fell to its lot in the nineteenth century. It was a policy designed to preserve the existence of his country. Churchill, by refusing to come to terms with me, has condemned his country to a policy of suicide. He has made the same mistakes as those generals make who wage a war according to the principles of the preceding war. There are now elements which it is impossible to fit into such a scheme of things. The crucial new factor is the existence of those two giants, the United States and Russia. Pitt's England ensured the balance of world power by preventing the hegemony of Europe—by preventing Napoleon, that is, from attaining his goal. Churchill's England, on the other hand, should have allowed the unification of Europe, if it wished to preserve that same balance of power.

At the beginning of this war I did my utmost to act as though I believed Churchill to be capable of grasping the truth of this great policy; and in his lucid moments he was, indeed, capable of grasping it. But for a long time now he has been bound hand and foot to the Jewish chariot. My object in trying to come to terms with England was to avoid creating an irreparable situation in the West. Later, when I attacked eastwards and lanced the Communist abscess, I hoped thereby to rekindle a spark of common sense in the minds of the Western Powers. I gave them the chance, without lifting a finger, of making a contribution to an act of catharsis, in which they could have safely left the task of disinfecting the West in our hands alone. But the hatred felt by these hypocrites for a man of good faith is stronger than their sense of self-preservation. I had underestimated the power of Jewish domination over Churchill's England. They preferred, indeed, to perish by default, rather than to admit National Socialism to their midst. Under pressure, they might have tolerated a façade of anti-semitism on our part. But our absolute determination to eradicate Jewish power root and branch throughout the world was far too strong meat for their delicate stomachs to digest!

Pitt's genius lay in the implementation of a realistic policy, in harmony with the conditions of the epoch, which allowed his country to make a truly extraordinary recovery and which ensured for it world supremacy in the nineteenth century. The servile imitation of this policy which Churchill is now pursuing—and with a complete disregard for the fact that conditions are not in the least the same—is a sheer absurdity. The fact is that the world has progressed since Pitt's day! For a whole century, changes, it is true, came slowly; but the first war increased the pace, and this war has led us to a presentation of the bills and a final settlement!

At the beginning of the nineteenth century, from the point of power, Europe alone counted. The great Asiatic empires had fallen into a sleep that resembled the sleep of death. The New World was still nothing more than an excrescence on the end of the old, and no one could reasonably have foreseen the prodigious destiny which awaited the thirteen British colonies which had just gained their freedom. . . . Thirteen! I'm not superstitious, but that story tempts me to become so! That new State of four million inhabitants, which grew so immeasurably in the

31

course of a hundred years that at the beginning of the twentieth century it had already become a world Power . . . !

During the decisive period between 1930 and 1940, the situation was quite different from that which obtained at the time of Pitt and Napoleon. Europe, exhausted by a great war, had lost her pride of place, and her role as leader was no longer recognized. It was still one of the centres of attraction on earth, but one which was steadily losing its importance in the face of the growing might of the United States of America, of the Russo-Asiatic colossus and of the Empire of the Rising Sun.

If fate had granted to an ageing and enfeebled Britain a new Pitt instead of this Jew-ridden, half-American drunkard, the new Pitt would at once have recognized that Britain's traditional policy of balance of power would now have to be applied on a different scale, and this time on a worldwide scale. Instead of maintaining, creating and adding fuel to European rivalries Britain ought to do her utmost to encourage and bring about a unification of Europe. Allied to a united Europe, she would then still retain the chance of being able to play the part of arbiter in world affairs.

Everything that is happening makes one think that Providence is now punishing Albion for her past crimes, the crimes which raised her to the power she was. The advent of Churchill, at a period that is decisive for both Britain and Europe, is the punishment chosen by Providence. For the degenerate *élite* of Britain, he's just the very man they want; and it is in the hands of this senile clown to decide the fate of a vast empire and, at the same time, of all Europe. It is, I think, an open question whether the British people, in spite of the degeneration of the aristocracy, has preserved those qualities which have hitherto justified British world domination. For my own part, I doubt it, because there does not seem to have been any popular reaction to the errors committed by the nation's leaders. And yet there have been many occasions when Britain could well have boldly set forth on a new and more fruitful course.

Had she so wished, Britain could have put an end to the war at the beginning of 1941. In the skies over London she had demonstrated to all the world her will to resist, and on her credit side she had the humiliating defeats which she had inflicted on the Italians in North Africa. The traditional Britain would have made peace. But the Jews would have none of it. And their lackeys, Churchill and Roosevelt, were there to prevent it.

Peace then, however, would have allowed us to prevent the Americans from meddling in European affairs. Under the guidance of the Reich, Europe would speedily have become unified. Once the Jewish poison had been eradicated, unification would have been an easy matter. France and Italy, each defeated in turn at an interval of a few months by the two Germanic Powers, would have been well out of it. Both would have had to renounce their inappropriate aspirations to greatness. At the same time they would have had to renounce their pretensions in North Africa and the Near East; and that would have allowed Europe to pursue a bold policy of friendship towards

Islam. As for Britain, relieved of all European cares, she could have devoted herself to the wellbeing of her Empire. And lastly, Germany, her rear secure, could have thrown herself heart and soul into her essential task, the ambition of my life and the *raison d'être* of National Socialism—the destruction of Bolshevism. This would have entailed the conquest of wide spaces in the East, and these in their turn would have ensured the future wellbeing of the German people.

The laws of nature follow a logic which does not necessarily always conform to our own ideas of logic. We ourselves were disposed to compromise. We were ready to throw our forces into the scales for the preservation of the British Empire; and all that, mark you, at a time when, to tell the truth, I feel much more sympathetically inclined to the lowliest Hindu than to any of these arrogant islanders. Later on, the Germans will be pleased that they did not make any contribution to the survival of an out-dated state of affairs for which the world of the future would have found it hard to forgive them. We can with safety make one prophecy: whatever the outcome of this war, the British Empire is at an end. It has been mortally wounded. The future of the British people is to die of hunger and tuberculosis in their cursed island.

British obstinacy and the desperate resistance being put up by the Reich have nothing in common. In the first place Britain had a freedom of choice, and nothing forced her to go to war. Yet, not only did she go to war, but she actually provoked war. I need hardly say that the Poles, had they not been urged on by the British and French warmongers (who were themselves spurred on by the Jews), would certainly not have felt themselves called upon to commit suicide. Even so, and even after having made this initial error, Britain could have pulled her chestnuts out of the fire, either after the liquidation of Poland or after the defeat of France. It would not, of course, have been very honourable on her part to do so; but in matters of this kind, the British sense of honour is not too particular. All she had to do was to place the blame for her defection squarely on the shoulders of her ex-allies—just as she and France did with Belgium in 1940, and, furthermore, we ourselves would have helped her to save face.

At the beginning of 1941, after her successes in North Africa had re-established her prestige, she had an even more favourable opportunity of withdrawing from the game and concluding a negotiated peace with us. Why, you may well ask, did she prefer to obey the orders of her Jewish and American allies, people, indeed, who were more voracious than even the worst of her enemies? I will tell you; Britain was not waging her own war, she was waging that which had been imposed on her by her implacable allies.

Germany, on the other hand, had no option. Once we had declared our desire of at last uniting all Germans in one great Reich and of ensuring for them a real independence—in other words, freedom to live their own lives—all our enemies at once rose against us. War became inevitable if for no other reason that in order to avoid it we should have been compelled to betray the fundamental interests of the German people. As far as our people were concerned we could not and would not be content with the mere semblance of independence. That sort of thing is all right for the Swedes and the Swiss, who are always prepared to subscribe to dubious and tortuous formulae, provided that they can at the same time line their pockets. Nor, for that matter could the Weimar Republic lay claim to any more worthy pretensions. That, however, is not an ambition worthy of the Third Reich.

We were, then, condemned to wage war—some time or other; and our sole preoccupation was to choose the least unfavourable moment. And once we were committed, of course, there could be no question of a withdrawal. It is not to the doctrines of National Socialism alone that our adversaries take exception. They hate National Socialism because through it the qualities of the German people have been exalted. They therefore seek the destruction of the German people—of that there can be no shadow of doubt. For once in a way, hatred has proved to be stronger than hypocrisy. We can only express our thanks to our enemies for having thus clearly exposed their minds to us.

To this all-embracing hatred we can retort only by means of total war. Fighting for our very survival, we are fighting desperately; and, whatever happens, we shall fight to the death to save our lives. Germany will emerge from this war stronger than ever before, and Britain more enfeebled than ever.

History shows that for Germany misfortune and adversity often constitute an indispensable prelude to a great renaissance. The sufferings of the German people—and in this war they have suffered incomparably more than any other people—are the very things which, if Providence wills, will help us to rise superior to the heady influence of victory. And should Providence abandon us, in spite of our sacrifices and our resolute steadfastness, it only means that Fate is subjecting us to ever greater trials, in order to give us the chance to confirm our right to live.

II

The last quarter of an hour—The determination to exterminate Germany—Leonidas and his three hundred Spartans—The miraculous death of the Tsarina, Elizabeth—Victory in the final sprint—This war started on 30th January 1933

6th February 1945

After fifty-four months of titanic struggle, waged on both sides with unexampled fury, the German people now finds itself alone, facing a coalition sworn to destroy it.

War is raging everywhere along our frontiers. It is coming closer and ever closer. Our enemies are gathering all their forces for the final assault. Their object is not merely to defeat us in battle but to crush and annihilate us. Their object is to destroy our Reich, to sweep our *Weltanschauung* from the face of the earth, to enslave the German people—as a punishment for their loyalty to National Socialism. We have reached the final quarter of an hour.

38

The situation is serious, very serious. It seems even to be desperate. We might very easily give way to fatigue, to exhaustion, we might allow ourselves to become discouraged to an extent that blinds us to the weaknesses of our enemies. But these weaknesses are there, for all that. We have facing us an incongruous coalition, drawn together by hatred and jealousy and cemented by the panic with which the National Socialist doctrine fills this Jew-ridden motley. Face to face with this amorphous monster, our one chance is to depend on ourselves and ourselves alone; to oppose this heterogeneous rabble with a national, homogeneous entity, animated by a courage which no adversity will be able to shake. A people which resists as the German people is now resisting can never be consumed in a witches' cauldron of this kind. On the contrary; it will emerge from the crucible with its soul more steadfast, more intrepid than ever. Whatever reverses we may suffer in the days that lie ahead of us, the German people will draw fresh strength from them; and whatever may happen today, it will live to know a glorious tomorrow.

The will to exterminate which goads these dogs in the pursuit of their quarry gives us no option; it indicates the path which we must follow—the only path that remains open to us. We must continue the struggle with the fury of desperation and without a glance over our shoulders; with our faces always to the enemy, we must defend step by step the soil of our fatherland. While we keep fighting, there is always hope, and that, surely, should be enough to forbid us to think that all is already lost. No game is lost until the final whistle. And if, in spite of everything, the Fates have decreed that we should once more in the course of our history be crushed by forces superior to our own, then let us go down with our heads high and secure in the knowledge that the honour of the German people remains without blemish. A desperate fight remains for all time a shining example. Let us remember Leonidas and his three hundred Spartans! In any case, we are not of the stuff that goes tamely to the slaughter like sheep. They may well exterminate us. But they will never lead us to the slaughter house!

No! There is no such thing as a desperate situation! Think how many examples of a turn of fortune the history of the German people affords! During the Seven Years' War Frederick found himself reduced to desperate straits. During the winter of 1762 he had decided that if no change occurred by a certain date fixed by himself, he would end his life by taking poison. Then, a few days before the date he had chosen, behold, the Tsarina died unexpectedly, and the whole situation was miraculously reversed. Like the great Frederick, we, too, are combating a coalition, and a coalition, remember, is not a stable entity. It exists only by the will of a handful of men. If Churchill were suddenly to disappear, everything could change in a flash! The British aristocracy might perhaps become conscious of the abyss opening before them—and might well experience a serious shock! These British, for whom, indirectly, we have been fighting and who would enjoy the fruits of our victory. . . .

We can still snatch victory in the final sprint! May we be granted the time to do so!

All we must do is to refuse to go down. For the German people, the simple fact of continued independent life would be a victory. And that alone would be sufficient justification for this war, which would not have been in vain. It was in any case unavoidable; the enemies of German National Socialism forced it upon me as long ago as January 1933.

III

Colonial enterprises exhaust a nation's strength—The new worlds are only excrescences on the old—The white races suffer a set-back—Materialism, alcoholism, fanaticism and syphilis—Unnatural sons—Germany's sole possible direction for expansion eastwards—Europe for the Europeans—The super-abundance of prolific Asia

7th February 1945

Any people which desires to prosper should remain linked to its own soil. A man should never lose contact with the soil upon which he had the honour of being born. He should not go away except for a short while and always with the intention of returning. The British who became colonizers of necessity, and who, indeed, were great colonizers, have generally obeyed this rule.

As far as continental people are concerned, I am sure that it is important that they should expand only in those directions where it is certain that the soil of conquerors and conquered are contiguous.

This need to become properly enrooted applies to all continental peoples and particularly, in my opinion, to the German people. And that most probably explains why we have never really felt the urge to become colonizers. A glance at history, both ancient and modern, will show that overseas enterprises have always in the long run impoverished those who undertook them. They have all, in the end, been exhausted by their efforts; and, in the inevitable nature of things, they have all succumbed to forces to which either they have themselves given birth or which they have themselves re-awakened. What better example of this than the Greeks?

What was true for the ancient Greeks remains equally true for all Europeans in modern times. To prosper, a people must concentrate its efforts on its own country. A scrutiny of any reasonably long period of history will reveal facts which confirm the truth of this contention.

Spain, France and Britain have all enfeebled, devitalized and drained themselves in these vain colonial enterprises. The continents to which Spain and Britain gave birth, which they created piece by piece, have today acquired a completely independent way of life and a completely egoistical outlook. Even so, they are but artificial worlds, with neither a soul, a culture nor a civilization of their own; and, judged from that point of view, they are nothing more than excrescences.

It is, of course, possible to make out a case for the success achieved in peopling continents which before had been empty. The United States and Australia afford good examples. Success, certainly—but only on the material

43

side. They are artificial edifices, bodies without age, of which it is impossible to say whether they are still in a state of infancy or whether they have already been touched by senility. In those continents which were inhabited, failure has been even more marked. In them, the white races have imposed their will by force, and the influence they have had on the native inhabitants has been negligible; the Hindus have remained Hindus, the Chinese have remained Chinese, and the Moslems are still Moslems. There have been no profound transformations, and such changes as have occurred are less marked in the religious field, notwithstanding the tremendous efforts of the Christian missionaries, than in any other. There have been a few odd conversions the sincerity of which are open to considerable doubt—except, perhaps, in the case of a few simpletons and mentally deficients. The white races did, of course, give some things to the natives, and they were the worst gifts that they could possibly have made, those plagues of our own modern world—materialism, fanaticism, alcoholism and syphilis. For the rest, since these peoples possessed qualities of their own which were superior to anything we could offer them, they have remained essentially unchanged. Where imposition by force was attempted, the results were even more disastrous, and common sense, realizing the futility of such measures, should preclude any recourse to their introduction. One solitary success must be conceded to the colonizers: everywhere they have succeeded in arousing hatred, a hatred that urges these peoples, awakened from their slumbers by us, to rise and drive us out. Indeed, it looks almost as though they had awakened solely and simply for that purpose! Can anyone assert that colonization has increased the number of Christians in the world? Where are those conversions *en masse* which mark the success of Islam? Here and there one finds isolated islets of Christians, Christians in name, that is, rather than by conviction; and that is the sum total of the successes of this magnificent Christian religion, the guardian of supreme Truth!

Taking everything into consideration, Europe's policy of colonization has ended in a complete failure. I have not forgotten the one instance of apparent success, but a success that is purely material, and it is of that monster which calls itself the United States that I wish to talk. And monster is the only possible name for it! At a time when the whole of Europe—their own mother—is fighting desperately to ward off the bolshevist peril, the United States, guided by the Jew-ridden Roosevelt, can think of nothing better to do than to place their fabulous material resources at the disposal of these Asiatic barbarians, who are determined to strangle her. Looking back, I am deeply distressed at the thought of those millions of Germans, men of good faith, who emigrated to the United States and who are now the backbone of the country. For these men, mark you, are not merely good Germans, lost to their fatherland; rather, they have become enemies, more implacably hostile than any others. The German emigrant retains, it is true, his qualities of industry and hard work, but he very quickly loses his soul. There is nothing more unnatural than a German who has become an expatriate.

In the future we must guard against these haemorrhages

45

of German blood. It is eastwards, only and always eastwards, that the veins of our race must expand. It is the
direction which Nature herself has decreed for the expansion of the German peoples. The rigorous climate with
which the East confronts them allows them to retain their
qualities as hardy and virile men; and the vivid contrasts
they find there help to keep fresh their love and their
longing for their own country. Transplant a German to
Kiev, and he remains a perfect German. But transplant
him to Miami, and you make a degenerate of him—in
other words, an American.

Since colonization is not an activity which Germans
feel called upon to pursue, Germany should never make
common cause with the colonizing nations and should
always abstain from supporting them in their colonial
aspirations. What we want is a Monroe doctrine in
Europe. 'Europe for the Europeans!', a doctrine, the
corollary of which should be that Europeans refrain from
meddling in the affairs of other continents.

The descendants of the convicts in Australia should
inspire in us nothing but a feeling of supreme indifference.
If their vitality is not strong enough to enable them to in-
crease at a rate proportionate to the size of the territories
they occupy, that is their own look out, and it is no use
their appealing to us for help. For my own part, I have no
objection at all to seeing the surplus populations of prolific
Asia being drawn, as to a magnet, to their empty spaces.
Let them all work out their own salvation! And let me
repeat—it is nothing to do with us.

IV

Should Franco have been drawn into the war?—Our involuntary contribution to the victory of the Spanish clergy—Irrevocable decadence of the Latin races—We ought to have occupied Gibraltar

10th February 1945

I have sometimes asked myself whether we were not wrong, in 1940, not to have drawn Spain into the war. It would have been too easy for words to do so, for Spain was burning to follow Italy's example and become a member of the Victors' Club.

Franco, of course, had very exaggerated ideas on the value of Spanish intervention. Nevertheless I believe that, in spite of the systematic sabotage perpetrated by his Jesuit brother-in-law, he would have agreed to make common cause with us on quite reasonable conditions—the promise of a little bit of France as a sop to his pride and a substantial slice of Algeria as a real, material asset. But as Spain had really nothing tangible to contribute, I

47

came to the conclusion that her direct intervention was not desirable. It is true that it would have allowed us to occupy Gibraltar. On the other hand, Spain's entry into the war would certainly have added many kilometres to the Atlantic coast-line which we would have had to defend —from Saint Sebastian to Cadiz. Then there was the further possibility of a renewal of the civil war, fanned by the British. We might thus have found ourselves bound for better or for worse to a régime for which I have now, if possible, less sympathy than ever, a régime of capitalist profiteers, puppets of the clerical gang! I shall never forgive Franco for not having reconciled the Spaniards once the civil war was over, for having ostracized the Phalangists, whom Spain has to thank for such aid as we gave her, and for having treated like bandits former foes, who were very far from all being Reds. To put half a country beyond the pale of the law while a minority of pillagers enrich themselves, with the blessing of the priest-hood, at the expense of the rest is no solution at all. I am quite sure that very few of the so-called Reds in Spain were really Communists. We were badly deceived, for, had I known the real state of affairs, I would never have allowed our aircraft to bombard and destroy a starving population and at the same time re-establish the Spanish clergy in all their horrible privileges.

To sum up, by ensuring that the Iberian peninsula remained neutral, Spain has already rendered us the one service in this conflict which she had in her power to render. Having Italy on our backs is a sufficient burden in all conscience; and whatever may be the qualities of the

Spanish soldier, Spain herself, in her state of poverty and unpreparedness, would have been a heavy liability rather than an asset.

This war will, I think, have clearly demonstrated at least one thing—the irremediable decadence of the Latin countries. They have shown beyond dispute that they are no longer in the running and that they therefore no longer have the right to participate in the settlement of the world's affairs.

The easiest thing would have been to occupy Gibraltar with our Commandos and with Franco's connivance, but without any declaration of war on his part. I am convinced that Britain would not have seized this as a pretext for declaring war on Spain. She would have been only too pleased to see Spain continue to remain non-belligerent. And from our own point of view, this would have eliminated all danger of any British landing on the coasts of Portugal.

V

Facing the Jewish problem with realism—The stranger who cannot be assimilated—A typically Jewish war—Exit the furtive Jew and enter Judea gloriosa—While Jews exist there will always be anti-semitism—The futility of racial hatred—Cross-breeding a failure—Prussian pride justified—The Atticism of the Austrians —The modern German type—In reality there is no such thing as a Jewish race—Superiority of mind over body—My honesty in dealing with the Jews

13th February 1945

It is one of the achievements of National Socialism that it was the first to face the Jewish problem in a realistic manner.

The Jews themselves have always aroused anti-semitism. Throughout the centuries, all the peoples of the world, from the ancient Egyptians to ourselves, have reacted in exactly the same way. The time comes when they become tired of being exploited by the disgusting Jew. They give a heave and shake themselves, like an animal trying to rid itself of its vermin. They react brutally and finally they revolt. It is an instinctive reaction, a reaction of repugnance against a stranger who refuses to adapt himself and become part of the whole, a parasite which clings to the host, imposes on it and exploits it to the utmost. By nature, the Jew is a parasite which cannot and will not be assimilated. A distinguishing feature of the Jew is that, unlike other foreigners, he everywhere claims all the rights of citizenship in the community that shelters him—and at the same time remains always a Jew. He regards it as his right to be allowed to run with the hare and hunt with the hounds; and he is the only man in the whole world to claim such an extravagant privilege.

National Socialism has tackled the Jewish problem by action and not by words. It has risen in opposition to the Jewish determination to dominate the world; it has attacked them everywhere and in every sphere of activity; it has flung them out of the positions they have usurped; it has pursued them in every direction, determined to purge the German world of the Jewish poison. For us, this has been an essential process of disinfection, which we have prosecuted to its ultimate limit and without which we should ourselves have been asphyxiated and destroyed.

With the success of the operation in Germany, there was a good chance of extending it further afield. This was, in fact, inevitable, for good health normally triumphs over disease. Quick to realize the danger, the Jews decided to stake their all in the life and death struggle which they launched against us. National Socialism had to be destroyed, whatever the cost and even if the whole world were destroyed in the process. Never before has there been a war so typically and at the same time so exclusively Jewish.

I have at least compelled them to discard their masks. And even if our endeavours should end in failure, it will only be a temporary failure. For I have opened the eyes of the whole world to the Jewish peril.

One of the consequences of our attitude has been to cause the Jew to become aggressive. As a matter of fact, he is less dangerous in that frame of mind than when he is sly and cunning. The Jew who openly avows his race is a hundred times preferable to the shameful type which claims to differ from you only in the matter of religion. If I win this war, I shall put an end to Jewish world power and I shall deal the Jews a mortal blow from which they will not recover. But if I lose the war, that does not by any means mean that their triumph is assured, for then they themselves will lose their heads. They will become so arrogant that they will evoke a violent reaction against them. They will, of course, continue to run with the hare and hunt with the hounds, to claim the privileges of citizenship in every country and, without sacrificing their pride, continue to remain, above all, members of the Chosen Race. The shifty, the shamefaced Jew will disappear and will be replaced by a Jew vainglorious and bombastic; and the latter will stink just as objectionably as the former—and perhaps even more so. There is, then, no danger in the circumstances that anti-semitism will disappear, for it is the Jews themselves who add fuel to its flames and see that it is kept well stoked. Before the opposition to it can disappear, the malady itself must disappear. And from that point of view, you can rely on the Jews: as long as they survive, anti-semitism will never fade.

In saying this, I promise you I am quite free of all racial hatred. It is, in any case, undesirable that one race should mix with other races. Except for a few gratuitous successes, which I am prepared to admit, systematic cross-breeding has never produced good results. Its desire to remain racially pure is a proof of the vitality and good health of a race. Pride in one's own race—and that does not imply contempt for other races—is also a normal and healthy sentiment. I have never regarded the Chinese or the Japanese as being inferior to ourselves. They belong to ancient civilizations, and I admit freely that their past history is superior to our own. They have the right to be proud of their past, just as we have the right to be proud of the civilization to which we belong. Indeed, I believe the more steadfast the Chinese and the Japanese remain in their pride of race, the easier I shall find it to get on with them.

This pride of race is a quality which the German, fundamentally, does not possess. The reason for this is that for these last three centuries the country has been torn by internal dissension and religious wars and has been subjected to a variety of foreign influences, to the influence, for example, of Christianity—for Christianity is not a natural religion for the Germans, but a religion that has been imported and which strikes no responsive chord in their hearts and is foreign to the inherent genius of the race. When pride of race manifests itself in a German, as it sometimes does and in a most aggressive form, it is in reality nothing more than a compensatory reaction for that inferiority complex from which so many Germans suffer. This, I need hardly say, does not apply to the Prussians. From the time of Frederick the Great they have possessed that quiet and simple pride which is the hall-mark of people who are sure of themselves and who have no need of ostentation to bear witness to what they are. Thanks to those qualities which are inherently theirs, the Prussians were able, as they well showed, to create a united Germany. National Socialism has tried to give to all Germans that pride which hitherto has been possessed by the Prussians alone among us.

The Austrians, too, have in their blood a pride very akin to that of the Prussians, a pride born of the fact that for centuries they have never been dominated by any other race, but have, on the contrary, been for a very long time the ones who gave orders and were obeyed. They possess the accumulated experience of domination and power, and to that is attributable that *panache* of Atticism which no one can gainsay.

In its crucible National Socialism will melt and fuse all those qualities which are characteristic of the German soul; and from it will emerge the modern German—industrious, conscientious, sure of himself yet simple withal, proud not of himself or what he is, but of his membership of a great entity which will evoke the admiration of other peoples. This feeling of corporate superiority does not in

54

any way imply the slightest desire to crush and overwhelm others. We have, I know, on occasions exaggerated our cult of this sentiment, but that was necessary at the outset and we were compelled to jostle the Germans pretty roughly in order to set their feet on the right road. In the nature of things, too violent a thrust in any direction invariably provokes an equally violent thrust in the opposite direction. All this, of course, cannot be accomplished in a day. It requires the slow-moving pressure of time. Frederick the Great is the real creator of the Prussian type. In actual fact, two or three generations elapsed before the type crystallized and before the Prussian type became a characteristic common to every Prussian.

Our racial pride is not aggressive except in so far as the Jewish race is concerned. We use the term Jewish race as a matter of convenience, for in reality and from the genetic point of view there is no such thing as the Jewish race. There does, however, exist a community, to which, in fact, the term can be applied and the existence of which is admitted by the Jews themselves. It is the spiritually homogeneous group, to membership of which all Jews throughout the world deliberately adhere, regardless of their whereabouts and of their country of domicile; and it is this group of human beings to which we give the title Jewish race. It is not, mark you, a religious entity, although the Hebrew religion serves them as a pretext to present themselves as such; nor indeed is it even a collection of groups, united by the bonds of a common religion.

The Jewish race is first and foremost an abstract race of the mind. It has its origins, admittedly, in the Hebrew religion, and that religion, too, has had a certain influence in moulding its general characteristics; for all that, however, it is in no sense of the word a purely religious entity, for it accepts on equal terms both the most determined atheists and the most sincere, practising believers. To all this must be added the bond that has been forged by centuries of persecution—though the Jews conveniently forget that it is they themselves who provoked these persecutions. Nor does Jewry possess the anthropological characteristics which would stamp them as a homogeneous race. It cannot, however, be denied that every Jew in the world has some drops of purely Jewish blood in him. Were this not so, it would be impossible to explain the presence of certain physical characteristics which are permanently common to all Jews from the ghetto of Warsaw to the bazaars of Morocco—the offensive nose, the cruel vicious nostrils and so on.

A race of the mind is something more solid, more durable than just a race, pure and simple. Transplant a German to the United States and you turn him into an American. But the Jew remains a Jew wherever he goes, a creature which no environment can assimilate. It is the characteristic mental make-up of his race which renders him impervious to the processes of assimilation. And there in a nutshell is the proof of the superiority of the mind over the flesh! . . .

The quite amazing ascendancy which they achieved during the course of the nineteenth century gave the Jews a sense of their own power and caused them to drop the mask; and it is just that that has given us the chance to oppose them as Jews, self-proclaimed and proud of the fact. And when you remember how credulous the Germans are, you will realize that we must be most grateful for this sudden excess of frankness on the part of our most mortal enemies.

I have always been absolutely fair in my dealings with the Jews. On the eve of war, I gave them one final warning. I told them that, if they precipitated another war, they would not be spared and that I would exterminate the vermin throughout Europe, and this time once and for all. To this warning they retorted with a declaration of war and affirmed that wherever in the world there was a Jew, there, too, was an implacable enemy of National Socialist Germany.

Well, we have lanced the Jewish abscess; and the world of the future will be eternally grateful to us.

VI

Too soon and too late—We lack time, because we lack space—A revolutionary State, pursuing a petit bourgeois policy—Collaboration with France was a mistake—We should have emancipated the French proletariat and liberated the French colonies—I was right in Mein Kampf

14th February 1945

The disastrous thing about this war is the fact that for Germany it began both too soon and too late. From the purely military point of view, it would have suited us better if it had started sooner. I ought to have seized the initiative in 1938 instead of allowing myself to be forced into war in 1939; for war was, in any case, unavoidable. However, you can hardly blame me if the British and the French accepted at Munich every demand I made of them!

As things stand at the moment, then, the war came a little too late. But from the point of view of our moral preparedness, it has come far too soon. My disciples have not yet had time to attain their full manhood. I should really have had another twenty years in which to bring this new *élite* to maturity, an *élite* of youth, immersed from infancy in the philosophy of National Socialism. The tragedy for us Germans is that we never have enough time. Circumstances always conspire to force us to hurry. And if at this point time is lacking, it is primarily because we lack space. The Russians with their vast expansion can afford the luxury of refusing to be hurried. Time works in their favour, but against us. Even if Providence had allotted to me a span of life sufficiently long to allow me to lead my people to the complete degree of development that National Socialism desires, you may be quite sure that our enemies would never have permitted me to take advantage of it. They would have done their utmost to destroy us before they found themselves face to face with a Germany, cemented by a single faith and National Socialist in body and soul, which would have been invincible.

Since we lacked men moulded in the shape of our ideal, we had perforce to make what use we could of those whom we had. The result has been obvious. Thanks to this discrepancy between conception and realization, the war policy of a revolutionary state like the Third Reich has of necessity been the policy of petty bourgeois reactionaries. Our generals and diplomats, with a few, rare exceptions, are men of another age; and their methods of waging war and of conducting our foreign policy also belong to an age that is passed. This is just as true of those who serve us in all good faith as it is of the rest of them. The former serve us ill through lack either of aptitude or enthusiasm, and the latter do so deliberately and of malice aforethought.

Our greatest political blunder has been our treatment of the French. We should never have collaborated with them. It is a policy which has stood them in good stead and has served us ill. Abetz thought he was being very clever when he became the champion of this idea and persuaded us to pursue it. He thought he was two moves ahead of events, whereas in reality he was well behind them. He seemed to think that we were dealing with the France of Napoleon, with a nation, that is, which was capable of appreciating the importance and far-reaching effects of a noble gesture. He failed to see what is an obvious fact, namely, that during the last hundred years France has changed completely. She has become a prostitute, and she is now a raddled old strumpet, who has never ceased to swindle and to confound us, and has always left us to foot the bill.

Our obvious course should have been to liberate the working classes and to help the workers of France to implement their own revolution. We should have brushed aside, rudely and without pity, the fossilized bourgeoisie, as devoid of soul as it is denuded of patriotism. Just look at the sort of friends our geniuses of the Wilhelmstrasse have found for us in France—petty, calculating little profiteers, who hastened to make love to us as soon as they thought that we were occupying their country in order to safeguard their bank balances—but who were quite resolved to betray us at the first possible opportunity, provided always that no danger to themselves was involved!

We were equally stupid as regards the French colonies. That, too, was the work of our great minds in the Wilhelmstrasse! Diplomats of the old, classic mould, soldiers of a bygone régime, petty country squires—of such were those who were to help us to revolutionize all Europe! And they have led us into waging war as they would have waged it in the nineteenth century. Never, at any price, should we have put our money on France and against the peoples subjected to her yoke. On the contrary, we should have helped them to achieve their liberty and, if necessary, should have goaded them into doing so. There was nothing to stop us in 1940 from making a gesture of this sort in the Near East and in North Africa. In actual fact our diplomats instead set about the task of consolidating French power, not only in Syria, but in Tunis, in Algeria and Morocco as well. Our 'gentlemen' obviously preferred to maintain cordial relations with distinguished Frenchmen, rather than with a lot of hirsute revolutionaries, with a chorus of musical comedy officers, whose one idea was to cheat us, rather than with the Arabs, who would have been loyal partners for us. Oh! you needn't think I don't see through the calculations of these Machiavellian professionals! They know their job and they have their traditions! All they thought about was the dirty trick they were playing on the British, for they were still under the ban of the famous alleged antagonism and rivalry between Britain and France in the colonial field. What I'm saying is perfectly true—they are still living in the reign of Wilhelm II, in the world of Queen Victoria and that of those artful sharpers named Poincaré and Delcassé! In actual fact this rivalry has ceased to be of any significance. That it still seems to exist is due to the fact that there are still some diplomats of the old school in the ranks of our adversaries too. In reality, Britain and France are associates, each of whom is playing his own game with considerable asperity, neither of whom react to any appeal to friendship, but both of whom unite again against a common danger. The Frenchman's deep-seated hatred of the German is something deeper and different. Therein lies a lesson on which we should do well to ponder in the future.

As regards France, there were two courses open to her. Either she could have abandoned her alliance with Britain, in which case she would have been of no interest to us as a potential ally, since we knew that she would also abandon us on the first opportunity; or she could have pretended to make this change of partners, in which case she would have been of even more dubious value to us. On our side, some of the wishful thinking about this country was quite ridiculous. In reality there was only one possible policy to adopt *vis-à-vis* France—a policy of rigorous and rigid distrust. I know I was right about France. With prophetic foresight I gave an accurate picture of France in *Mein Kampf*. And I know perfectly well why, in spite of all the representations that have been made to me, I have seen no reason at all to change the opinions I formed twenty years ago.*

* Hitler was frequently urged to suppress or to change the passage on France in the later editions of his book, *Mein Kampf*, but he consistently refused to do so—even after Munich. It is to this that he is alluding here.

VII

The gravest decision of the war—Peace with Britain not possible till the Red Army had been annihilated—Time works against us—Stalin's blackmail—Settlement with Russia as soon as the weather became fine

15th February 1945

No decision which I have had to make during the course of this war was graver than that to attack Russia. I had always maintained that we ought at all costs to avoid waging war on two fronts, and you may rest assured that I pondered long and anxiously over Napoleon and his experiences in Russia. Why, then, you may ask, this war against Russia, and why at the time that I selected?

We had already given up hope of ending the war by means of a successful invasion of Britain. Furthermore that country, under the guidance of its stupid chiefs, would have refused to recognize the hegemony we had set up in Europe as long as there remained on the Continent a Great Power which was fundamentally hostile to the Third Reich. The war, then, would have gone on and on, a war in which, behind the British, the Americans would have played an increasingly active role. The importance of the war potential of the United States, the progress made in armaments—both in our own camp and in that of our enemies, the proximity of the English coast—all these things combined to make it highly inadvisable for us to become bogged down in a war of long duration. For Time —and it's always Time, you notice—would have been increasingly against us. In order to persuade Britain to pack up, to compel her to make peace, it was essential to rob her of her hope of being able still to confront us, on the Continent itself, with an adversary of a stature equal to our own. We had no choice, we had at all costs to strike the Russian element out of the European balance sheet. We had another reason, equally valid, for our action—the mortal threat that a Russia in being constituted to our existence. For it was absolutely certain that one day or other she would attack us.

Our one and only chance of vanquishing Russia was to take the initiative, for to fight a defensive war against her was not practical. We dared not allow the Red Army the advantage of the terrain, place our *Autobahns* at the disposal of its swiftly on-rushing armour, and our railways at the disposal of its troops and its supplies. But if we took the offensive, we could, indeed, defeat the Red Army on its own ground, in the swamps and in the vast and muddy expanses; but in a civilized country we could not have done so. We should simply have been providing it with a spring-board with which to leap upon the whole of Europe and destroy it.

Why 1941? Because, in view of the steadily increasing power of our western enemies, if we were to act at all, we had to do so with the least possible delay. Nor, mind you, was Stalin doing nothing. On two fronts, time was against us. The real question was not, therefore: 'Why 22 June 1941 already' but rather: 'Why not earlier still?' But for the difficulties created for us by the Italians and their idiotic campaign in Greece, I should have attacked Russia a few weeks earlier. For us, the main problem was to keep the Russians from moving for as long as possible, and my own personal nightmare was the fear that Stalin might take the initiative before me.

Another reason was that the raw materials which the Russians were withholding were essential to us. In spite of their obligations their rate of delivery decreased steadily, and there was a real danger that they might suddenly cease altogether. If they were not prepared to give us of their own free will the things we had to have, then we had no alternative but to go and take them, *in situ* and by force. I came to my decision immediately after Molotov's visit to Berlin in November, for it then became clear to me that sooner or later Stalin would abandon us and go over to the enemy. Ought I to have played for time in order that our preparations could have become more complete? No—for by so doing I should have sacrificed the initiative; and again no, because the brief and precarious respite which we might have gained would have cost us very dear. We should have had to submit to the Soviet blackmail with regard to Finland, to Rumania, to Bulgaria and to Turkey. That, of course, was out of the question. The Third Reich, defender and protector of Europe, could not have sacrificed these friendly countries on the altar of Communism. Such behaviour would have been dishonourable, and we should have been punished for it. From the moral as well as from the strategic point of view it would have been a miserable gambit. War with Russia had become inevitable, whatever we did; and to postpone it only meant that we should later have to fight under conditions far less favourable.

I therefore decided, as soon as Molotov departed, that I would settle accounts with Russia as soon as fair weather permitted.

VIII

A people which instinctively dislikes colonial adventures
—Louisiana and Mexico

15th February 1945

By not liberating the French proletariat at once in 1940 we both failed in our duty and neglected our own interests. And that is equally true with regard to French subjects overseas.

The French people would certainly have borne us no grudge, had we relieved them of the burden of Empire. In this respect the people have shown much more common sense than the self-styled *élite*, and they have an instinctive and much truer appreciation of the nation's real interests. Under both Louis XV and under Jules Ferry the people revolted against the absurdity of colonial adventures. I have yet to be convinced that Napoleon became unpopular for having rid himself cheaply of Louisiana. But there was unprecedented indignation when his inefficient nephew tried to balance matters by waging war on Mexico!

IX

Some Frenchmen were courageous Europeans—The price of clear thinking and good faith

15th February 1945

I have never liked France or the French, and I have never stopped saying so. I admit, however, that there are some worthy men among them. There is no doubt that, during these latter years, quite a number of Frenchmen supported the European conception with both complete sincerity and great courage. And the savagery with which their own countrymen made them pay for their clear vision is of itself a proof of their good faith.

X

My attitude towards Italy a mistake—The Italian alliance a hindrance almost everywhere—We miss the political bus as regards Islam—Shameful defeats of the Italians—Italy will have contributed to our losing the war—Life does not forgive weakness

17th February 1945

When I pass judgment, objectively and without emotion, on events, I must admit that my unshakeable friendship for Italy and the Duce may well be held to be an error on my part. It is in fact quite obvious that our Italian alliance has been of more service to our enemies than to ourselves. Italian intervention has conferred benefits which are modest in the extreme in comparison with the numerous difficulties to which it has given rise. If, in spite of all our efforts, we fail to win this war, the Italian alliance will have contributed to our defeat!

The greatest service which Italy could have rendered to us would have been to remain aloof from this conflict. To ensure her abstention, no sacrifices, no presents on our part would have been too great. Had she steadfastly maintained her neutral role, we would have overwhelmed her with our favours. In victory we would have shared with her all the fruits and all the glory. We would have collaborated with all our hearts in the creation of the historic myth of the supremacy of the Italian people, the legitimate sons of the ancient Romans. Indeed, anything would have been preferable to having them as comrades in arms on the field of battle!

Italy's intervention in June 1940, with the sole purpose of aiming a donkey-kick at a French army that was already in process of disintegration, merely had the effect of tarnishing a victory which the vanquished were at the time prepared to accept in a sporting spirit. France recognized that she had been fairly defeated by the armies of the Reich, but she was unwilling to accept defeat at the hands of the Axis.

Our Italian ally has been a source of embarrassment to us everywhere. It was this alliance, for instance, which prevented us from pursuing a revolutionary policy in North Africa. In the nature of things, this territory was becoming an Italian preserve and it was as such that the Duce laid claim to it. Had we been on our own, we could have emancipated the Moslem countries dominated by France; and that would have had enormous repercussions in the Near East, dominated by Britain, and in Egypt. But with our fortunes linked to those of the Italians, the pursuit of such a policy was not possible. All Islam vibrated at the news of our victories. The Egyptians, the

Irakis and the whole of the Near East were all ready to rise in revolt. Just think what we could have done to help them, even to incite them, as would have been both our duty and in our own interest! But the presence of the Italians at our side paralysed us; it created a feeling of *malaise* among our Islamic friends, who inevitably saw in us accomplices, willing or unwilling, of their oppressors. For the Italians in these parts of the world are more bitterly hated, of course, than either the British or the French. The memories of the barbarous reprisals taken against the Senussi are still vivid. Then again the ridiculous pretensions of the Duce to be regarded as The Sword of Islam evokes the same sneering chuckle now as it did before the war. This title, which is fitting for Mahomed and a great conqueror like Omar, Mussolini caused to be conferred on himself by a few wretched brutes whom he had either bribed or terrorized into doing so. We had a great chance of pursuing a splendid policy with regard to Islam. But we missed the bus, as we missed it on several other occasions, thanks to our loyalty to the Italian alliance!

In this theatre of operations, then, the Italians prevented us from playing our best card, the emancipation of the French subjects and the raising of the standard of revolt in the countries oppressed by the British. Such a policy would have aroused the enthusiasm of the whole of Islam. It is a characteristic of the Moslem world, from the shores of the Atlantic to those of the Pacific, that what affects one, for good or for evil, affects all.

On the moral side, the effects of our policy were doubly

disastrous. On the one hand we had wounded, with no advantage to ourselves, the self-esteem of the French. On the other hand this, of itself, compelled us to maintain the domination exercised by the French over their empire, for fear that the contagion might spread to Italian North Africa and that the latter might then also claim its independence. And since all these territories are now occupied by the Anglo-Americans, I am more than justified in saying that this policy of ours was a disaster. Further, this futile policy has allowed those hypocrites, the British, to pose, if you please, as liberators in Syria, in Cyrenaica and in Tripolitania!

From the purely military point of view things have not been much better! Italy's entry into the war at once gave our enemies their first victories, a fact which enabled Churchill to revive the courage of his countrymen and which gave hope to all the Anglophiles all the world over. Even while they proved themselves incapable of maintaining their positions in Abyssinia and Cyrenaica, the Italians had the nerve to throw themselves, without seeking our advice and without even giving us previous warning of their intentions, into a pointless campaign in Greece. The shameful defeats which they suffered caused certain of the Balkan States to regard us with scorn and contempt. Here, and nowhere else, are to be found the causes of Yugoslavia's stiffening attitude and her *volte-face* in the spring of 1941. This compelled us, contrary to all our plans, to intervene in the Balkans, and that in its turn led to a catastrophic delay in the launching of our attack on Russia. We were compelled to expend some of our best divisions there. And as a net result we were then forced to occupy vast territories in which, but for this stupid show, the presence of any of our troops would have been quite unnecessary. The Balkan States would have been only too pleased, had they been so allowed, to preserve an attitude of benevolent neutrality towards us. As for our paratroopers I would have preferred to launch them against Gibraltar than against Corinth or Crete!

Ah! if only the Italians had remained aloof from this war! If only they had continued in their state of non-belligerence! In view of the friendship and the common interests that bind us, of what inestimable value to us such an attitude would have been! The Allies themselves would have been delighted, for, although they never held any very high opinion of the martial qualities of Italy, even they never dreamed that she would turn out to be as feeble as she was. They would have considered themselves lucky to see remain neutral such power as they attributed to the Italians. Even so, they could not have afforded to take chances, and they would have been compelled to immobilize considerable forces to meet the danger of an intervention, which was always menacing and which was always possible, if not probable. From our point of view this means that there would have been a considerable number of British troops, immobile and acquiring neither the experience of battle nor the fillip derived from victory—in short, a sort of 'phoney war', and the longer it continued, the greater would be the advantage that we gained from it.

A war that is prolonged is of benefit to a belligerent in

that it gives him the opportunities to learn to wage war. I had hoped to conduct this war without giving the enemy the chance of learning anything new in the art of battle. In Poland and Scandinavia, in Holland, Belgium and France I succeeded. Our victories were swift, were achieved with a minimum of casualties on both sides, but were yet sufficiently clear-cut and decisive to lead to the complete defeat of the enemy.

If the war had remained a war conducted by Germany, and not by the Axis, we should have been in a position to attack Russia by 15th May 1941. Doubly strengthened by the fact that our forces had known nothing but decisive and irrefutable victories, we should have been able to conclude the campaign before winter came. How differently everything has turned out!

Out of gratitude (for I shall never forget the attitude adopted by the Duce at the time of the Anschluss) I have always abstained from criticizing or passing judgment on Italy. I have on the contrary always been at great pains to treat her as an equal. Unfortunately, the laws of nature have shown that it is a mistake to treat as equals those who are not your equals. The Duce himself is my equal. He may perhaps even be my superior from the point of view of his ambitions for his people. But it is facts and not ambitions that count.

We Germans do well to remember that in circumstances such as these it is better for us to play a lone hand. We have everything to lose and nothing to gain by binding ourselves closely with more feeble elements and by choosing into the bargain partners who have given all too frequent proof of their fickleness. I have often said that wherever you find Italy, there you will find victory. What I should have said is—wherever you find victory, there, you may be sure, you will find Italy!

Neither my personal affection for the Duce nor my instinctive feelings of friendship for the Italian people have changed. But I do blame myself for not having listened to the voice of reason, which bade me to be ruthless in my friendship for Italy. And I could have done so, both to the personal advantage of the Duce himself and to the advantage of his people. I realize, of course, that such an attitude on my part would have offended him and that he would never have forgiven me. But as a result of my forbearance things have happened which should not have happened and which may well prove fatal. Life does not forgive weakness.

XI

A cast-iron excuse for Roosevelt—Nothing could have prevented the entry of the U.S.A. into the war—The Yellow Peril obsession—Solidarity with the Japanese

18th February 1945

Japan's entry into the war caused us no misgivings, even though it was obvious that the Japanese had made a present of a cast-iron pretext to Roosevelt for bringing in the United States against us. But Roosevelt, urged on by Jewry, was already quite resolved to go to war and annihilate National Socialism, and he had no need of any pretexts. Such pretexts as were required to overcome the resistance of the isolationists he was quite capable of fabricating for himself. One more little swindle meant nothing to him.

The magnitude of the Pearl Harbour disaster was, I am sure, balm to his soul. It was exactly what he wanted in order to be able to drag his countrymen into a total war and to annihilate the last remnants of opposition in his own country. He had done all in his power to provoke the Japanese. It was only a repetition, on a vaster scale, of the tactics employed with such success by Wilson at the time of the first war: the torpedoing of the *Lusitania*, provoked with diabolical skill, prepared the Americans psychologically for the entry of their country into the war against Germany. Since the intervention of the United States could not be prevented in 1917, it is obvious that their intervention now, twenty-five years later, was both a logical premise and unavoidable.

It was only in 1915 that World Jewry decided to place the whole of its resources at the disposal of the Allies. But in our case, Jewry decided as early as 1933, at the very birth of the Third Reich, tacitly to declare war on us. Furthermore the influence wielded by the Jews in the United States has consistently and steadily increased during the last quarter of a century. And since the entry of the United States into the war was quite inevitable, it was a slice of great good fortune for us to have at our side an ally of such great worth as Japan. But it was also a slice of great good fortune for the Jews. It gave them the chance they had so long been seeking to implicate the United States directly in the conflict, and it was a master stroke on their part to have succeeded in dragging the Americans unanimously and enthusiastically into their war. The Americans, mindful of their disillusionment in 1919, were by no means anxious once again to intervene in a European war. On the other hand they were more obsessed than ever with the idea of the Yellow Peril. Trying to teach the

Jews a trick or two is like carrying coals to Newcastle, and you can be quite sure that all their plans are conceived with Machiavellian astuteness. I myself am quite convinced that in the case we are discussing they took a very long view which envisaged the overthrow by a white Power of the Empire of the Rising Sun, which had risen to the status of a world Power and which had always sternly resisted contamination by the race of Jewry.

For us, Japan will always remain an ally and a friend. This war will teach us to appreciate and respect her more than ever. It will encourage us to draw more tightly the bonds which unite our two countries. It is of course regrettable that the Japanese did not enter the war against Russia and at the same time as ourselves. Had they done so, Stalin's armies would not now be besieging Breslau or squatting in Budapest. We should have liquidated Bolshevism by the time winter came, and Roosevelt would have hesitated to take on adversaries as powerful as our two selves. In the same way I am sorry that Japan did not capture Singapore as early as 1940, immediately after the defeat of France. The United States was then on the eve of a presidential election and would have found it impossible to intervene. That, then, was one of the turning points of the war.

In spite of everything, we and the Japanese will remain staunchly side by side. We will conquer or die together. Should we be the first to succumb, I can't see the Russians continuing to maintain the myth of 'Asiatic solidarity' for the sake of Japan!

XII

We should have occupied Gibraltar in 1940—Congenital weakness of the Latin countries—The British duped by the French—Misunderstandings with the Duce—The disastrous campaign in Greece

20th February 1945

Taking advantage of the enthusiasm we had aroused in Spain and the shock to which we had subjected Britain, we ought to have attacked Gibraltar in the summer of 1940, immediately after the defeat of France.

At that time, however, the awkward thing was that it would have been difficult to prevent Spain entering into the war on our side—and particularly so as we had failed, a few weeks previously, from preventing Italy from flying to the rescue of our victory.

These Latin countries bring us no luck. Their overweening conceit is in direct proportion to their weakness, and that always confuses the issue. We failed entirely to

79

curb the Italians' desire to shine on the field of battle, even though we had shown ourselves willing to confer upon them an honours degree for heroism, to bestow upon them all the fruits of military glory and all the advantages accruing from a war that has been won—provided always that they took no part in it at all.

The British, of course, were duped even more completely by their Latin ally than we were. Chamberlain, obviously, would never have declared war, had he realized the full extent of French demoralization and inadequacy. For the British undoubtedly expected France to bear the whole brunt of the land campaign on the Continent. For Chamberlain nothing would have been easier than to shed a few crocodile's tears for Poland and then to have left us to carve the country up at our leisure.

To material weakness the Latin countries add a quite fantastic pretentiousness. Friendly Italy or hostile France —it makes no odds. The weakness of both of them will have been equally fatal to us.

The only disagreements that have ever occurred between the Duce and myself arose from the precautions which from time to time I had felt constrained to take. In spite of the complete confidence I had in him personally, I felt compelled to keep him in ignorance of my intentions in any case where indiscretion might have prejudiced our interests. Just as I had complete confidence in Mussolini, he had complete confidence in Ciano—and he, of course, had no secrets from the pretty ladies who fluttered like butterflies around him. That we know to our cost, and as the enemy were anxious for information regardless of costs, they learnt a goodly number of secrets through this channel. I had good reasons, therefore, for not telling the Duce everything. I am only sorry that he did not appreciate the fact, that he resented my attitude and paid me back in my own coin.

There's no doubt about it—we have no luck with the Latin races! While I was occupied, first in Montoire, buttoning up a futile policy of collaboration with France, and then in Hendaye, where I had to submit to receiving fulsome honours at the hands of a false friend, a third Latin—and one, this time, who really was a friend—took advantage of my preoccupation to set in motion his disastrous campaign against Greece.

XIII

Third Reich's need of peace to consolidate—Abstract man and the Utopian doctrines—National Socialism a realistic doctrine, applicable only to Germany—Had war occurred in 1938, it would have been a local war—What would have happened—a double coup for the West

21st February 1945

We had need of peace in order to carry out our programme. I always desired to maintain peace. We have been jockeyed into war at the desire of our enemies. In practice, the threat of war has existed ever since January 1933, from the time that I came to power.

On the one hand, there are the Jews and all those who march in step with them. On the other, there are those who adopt a realistic attitude towards world affairs. And throughout history we have had these two families of wholly irreconcilable outlook in the world.

On the one hand, there are those who strive for the happiness of mankind in the abstract and who pursue the

82

chimera of a formula applicable all the world over. On the other, there are the realists. National Socialism is interested only in the happiness of the German race and strives only to secure the wellbeing of the German man.

The universalists, the idealists, the Utopians all aim too high. They give promises of an unattainable paradise, and by doing so they deceive mankind. Whatever label they wear, whether they call themselves Christians, Communists, humanitarians, whether they are merely sincere but stupid or wire-pullers and cynics, they are all makers of slaves. I myself have always kept my eye fixed on a paradise which, in the nature of things, lies well within our reach. I mean an improvement in the lot of the German people.

I have restricted myself to making promises that I knew I could keep and that I had every intention of keeping. Hence the universal hatred which I have aroused. By refusing to make impossible promises, as do our enemies, I was not playing the game. I was holding myself aloof from the syndicate of the world's leaders, whose aim, unavowed but tacitly accepted, is the exploitation of human credulity.

The National Socialist doctrine, as I have always proclaimed, is not for export. It was conceived for the German people. All the objectives at which it aims are, of necessity, limited—but attainable. It follows, then, that I can put as little credence in the idea of universal peace as in that of universal war.

It was on the eve of Munich that I realized beyond doubt that the enemies of the Third Reich were determined to have our hide at all costs and that there was no possibility of coming to terms with them. When that arch capitalist bourgeois, Chamberlain, with his deceptive umbrella in his hand, put himself to the trouble of going all the way to the Berghof to discuss matters with that upstart, Hitler, he knew very well that he really intended to wage ruthless war against us. He was quite prepared to tell me anything which he thought might serve to lull my suspicions. His one and only object in undertaking this trip was to gain time. What we ought then to have done was to have struck at once. We ought to have gone to war in 1938. It was the last chance we had of localizing the war.

But they gave way all along the line and, like the pol-troons that they are, ceded to all our demands. Under such conditions it was very difficult to seize the initiative and commence hostilities. At Munich we lost a unique opportunity of easily and swiftly winning a war that was in any case inevitable.

Although we were ourselves not fully prepared, we were nevertheless better prepared than the enemy. September 1938 would have been the most favourable date. And what a chance we had to limit the conflict.

We ought then and there to have settled our disputes by force of arms and disregarded the inclination of our opponents to meet all our demands. When we solved the Sudeten question by force we liquidated Czechoslovakia at the same time—and left all the blame squarely on Benes' shoulders. The Munich solution could not have been anything but provisional, for, obviously, we could not tolerate in the heart of Germany an abscess, small though it was, like an independent Czech state. We lanced the abscess in March 1939, but in circumstances that were psychologically less favourable than those which would have obtained had we settled the issue by force in 1938. For in March 1939, for the first time, we put ourselves in the wrong in the eyes of world opinion. No longer were we restricting ourselves to reuniting Germans to the Reich, but were establishing a protectorate over a non-German population.

A war waged in 1938 would have been a swift war—for the emancipation of the Sudeten Germans, the Slovaks, the Hungarians and even of those Poles who were under Czech domination. Great Britain and France taken by surprise and discountenanced by the course of events would have remained passive—particularly in view of the fact that world opinion would have been on our side. Finally, Poland, the main prop of French policy in eastern Europe, would have been at our side. If Great Britain and France had made war on us in these circumstances they would have lost face. In actual fact, I'm quite sure they would not have gone to war; but they would have lost face all the same. Once our arms had spoken, we could have left till later the settlement of the remaining territorial problems in eastern Europe and the Balkans without fear of provoking the intervention of the two Powers, already discredited in the eyes of their protégés. As far as we ourselves were concerned, we should thus have gained the time required to enable us to consolidate our position, and we would have postponed the world war for several years to come. In fact, in these circumstances I doubt very much whether a second world war would, indeed, have been inevitable.

It is by no means unreasonable to presume that in the breasts of the well-found nations degeneration and love of comfort could well have proved stronger than the congenital hatred they bore us—particularly when it is remembered that they must have realized that all our aspirations were, in reality, orientated eastwards. Our adversaries might even have deluded themselves with the hope that we might perhaps exhaust ourselves in the pursuit of these eastern aspirations of ours. In any event, it would, for them, have been a case of heads I win, tails you lose, since it would have ensured for them maintenance of peace in the west, and at the same time would have allowed them to take advantage of the resultant weakening of Russia, whose growing power had been a source of preoccupation for them, though to a lesser degree than had been our own resurgence.

XIV

The tragedy of war with America—Contribution by
Germans to America's greatness—The failure of the
New Deal and the war—Possibility of peaceful co-
existence between Germany and U.S.A.—The Americans will become anti-Jew—Roosevelt, a false idol—No
colonial ventures, but a grand Continental policy

24th February 1945

This war against America is a tragedy. It is illogical and
devoid of any foundation of reality.

It is one of those queer twists of history that just as I
was assuming power in Germany, Roosevelt, the elect of
the Jews, was taking command in the United States.
Without the Jews and without this lackey of theirs, things
could have been quite different. For from every point of
view Germany and the United States should have been
able, if not to understand each other and sympathize with
each other, then at least to support each other without
undue strain on either of them. Germany, remember, has

made a massive contribution to the peopling of America. It is we Germans who have made by far the greatest contribution of Nordic blood to the United States. And it is also a fact that Steuben played a part which decided the issue in the War of Independence.

The last great economic crisis struck Germany and the United States at more or less the same time and with the same force. Both countries rode the storm in much the same way. The operation, though extremely difficult, was crowned with success on our side. In America, where, after all, it presented no difficulty at all, the operation achieved only a very mediocre success under the guidance of Roosevelt and his Jewish advisers. The failure of the New Deal is responsible in no small measure for their war fever. The United States as a matter of fact could survive and prosper in a state of economic isolation; for us, that is a dream which we would love to see come true. They have at their disposal a vast territory, ample to absorb the energies of all their people. As far as Germany is concerned, my hope is one day to ensure for her complete economic independence inside a territory of a size compatible with her population. A great people has need of broad acres.

Germany expects nothing from the United States, and the latter have nothing to fear from Germany. Everything combines to ensure the possibility of peaceful co-existence, each in his own country and all in perfect harmony. Unfortunately, the whole business is ruined by the fact that world Jewry has chosen just that country in which to set up its most powerful bastion. That, and that alone, has altered the relations between us and has poisoned everything.

I am prepared to wager that well within twenty-five years the Americans themselves will have realized what a handicap has been imposed upon them by this parasitic Jewry, clamped fast to their flesh and nourishing itself on their life-blood. It is this Jewry that is dragging them into adventures which, when all is said and done, are no concern of theirs and in which the interests at stake are of no importance to them. What possible reason can the non-Jewish Americans have for sharing the hatreds of the Jews and following meekly in their footsteps? One thing is quite certain—within a quarter of a century the Americans will either have become violently anti-semitic or they will be devoured by Jewry.

If we should lose this war, it will mean that we have been defeated by the Jews. Their victory will then be complete. But let me hasten to add that it will only be very temporary. It will certainly not be Europe which takes up the struggle again against them, but it certainly will be the United States. The latter is a country still too young to have acquired the maturity conferred by age and exaggeratedly lacking in political sense. For the Americans, everything has so far been ridiculously easy. But experience and difficulties will perhaps cause them to mature. Just think for a moment what they were when their country was born—a group of individuals come from all corners of the earth hastening forward in pursuit of fortune and finding at their disposal a vast continent to appease their hunger and all theirs for the taking. National conscience is a thing which develops very gradually, especially in vast territories such as these. Nor must it be forgotten that these individuals had been drawn from a variety of races and had not yet been fused by the bonds of a national spirit. What an easy prey for the Jews!

The excesses in which the Jews indulged in our country are as nothing in comparison with the excesses in which they have indulged and in which they will continue to indulge in ever increasing measure on their new hunting grounds. It will not be very long before the Americans realize that the Roosevelt whom they have adored is an idol with feet of clay and that this Jew-ridden man is in reality a malefactor—both from the point of view of the United States and of humanity as a whole. He has dragged them along a path on which they had no business to be, and in particular he has forced them to take an active part in a conflict that does not concern them at all. Had they possessed even a minimum of political instinct they would have remained in their splendid isolation, content in this conflict to play the role of arbiter. Had they been a little more mature and a little more experienced, they would doubtless have realized that their best course in their own major interests would have been to have entrenched themselves firmly with their faces towards a shattered Europe and in an attitude of vigilant neutrality. By intervening they have once again played into the hands of their Jewish exploiters; and the latter are worldly wise and know exactly what they are doing—but, of course, from their own particular Jewish point of view.

Had Fate so willed that the President of the United

States during this critical period were someone other than Roosevelt, he might well have been a man capable of adapting the American economy to the needs of the twentieth century and of becoming the greatest President since Lincoln. The 1930 crisis was brought on by growing pains—but on a world-wide scale. Economic liberalism showed that it was nothing more than an out-dated catch-phrase. Once the signification and the potentialities of the crisis had been appreciated, all that was required was the discovery of appropriate remedies. That is the task on which a great President would have concentrated, and by so doing he would have placed his country in an unassail-able place in the world. Naturally a wise President should have fostered among his countrymen an interest in inter-national affairs and should have encouraged them to turn their eyes to the great world at large; but to have flung them into the middle of a dog fight, as this criminal, Roosevelt, has done, was sheer lunacy. He, of course, has quite cynically taken advantage of their ignorance, their naïveté and their credulity. He has made them see the world through the eye of Jewry, and he has set them on a path which will lead them to utter disaster, if they do not pull themselves together in time.

American affairs are no business of ours, and I should be completely indifferent to what happens to them, but for the fact that their attitude has direct repercussions on our destiny and on that of Europe.

The fact that neither we nor they have any colonial policy is yet another characteristic which should unite us. The Germans have never really felt the imperialist urge.

I regard the efforts made at the end of the nineteenth century as a fortuitous accident in our history. Our defeat in 1918 had at least the fortunate consequences that it stopped us from pursuing the course into which the Germans had foolishly allowed themselves to be led, influenced by the example of the French and the British and jealous of a success which they had not the wit to realize was purely transitory.

It is to the credit of the Third Reich that we did not look back with any nostalgia to a past that we have discarded. We have on the contrary turned our eyes resolutely and bravely towards the future, towards the creation of great homogeneous entities and a great Continental policy. It is, incidentally, a policy on all fours with the traditional American policy of not meddling in the affairs of other continents and forbidding others to meddle in the affairs of the New World.

XV

The Germans always, inevitably, in a hurry—Time
fights on Russia's side—A people with a tragic past—
Not the work of one man, or even of a generation—
Germans have never ceased to fight for their existence

25th February 1945

It is a fact that we always bungle everything through being
forced to act in a hurry. With us, to act swiftly is always to
act with precipitation. To acquire the gift of patience, we
should have both time and space, and at the moment we
have neither. The Russians are lucky in possessing both,
quite apart from that inclination towards placidity which
is a characteristic trait of the Slav temperament.

Furthermore, thanks to the Marxist religion, they have
everything required to make them patient. They have been
promised happiness on earth (a feature which distin-
guishes Marxism from the Christian religion)—but in the
future. The Jew, Mardochée Marx, like the good Jew that

93

he was, was awaiting the coming of the Messiah. He has placed the Messiah conception in a setting of historic materialism by asserting that terrestrial happiness is a factor in an almost endless process of evolution. 'Happiness is within your reach,' he says, 'that I promise you. But you must let evolution take its course and not try to hurry matters.' Mankind always falls for a specious trick of that sort. . . . Lenin did not have the time, but Stalin will carry on the good work, and so on and so on. . . . Marxism is a very powerful force. But how shall we assess Christianity, that other child of Judaism, which will not commit itself further than to promise the faithful happiness in another world? Believe me, it is incomparably stronger!

I myself am fated to being compelled to try to accomplish everything in the short space of a human lifetime. To help me I have but a realistic idealism, based on tangible facts, from which flows promises that can certainly be fulfilled, but which forbids me to promise the moon. Where others have all eternity at their disposal, I have but a few short, miserable years. Those others know that they will be succeeded by yet others who will carry on where they left off, ploughing with precision exactly the same furrow with exactly the same plough. I have now reached the stage where I wonder whether among my immediate successors there will be found a man predestined to raise and carry on the torch, when it has slipped from my hand.

It has also been my fate to be the servant of a people with so tragic a past, a people so unstable, so versatile as the German people, and a people who go, according to circumstances, from one extreme to the other. From my own point of view, the ideal thing would have been, firstly, to ensure the future existence of the German people, then to form a youth imbued deeply with the National Socialist doctrine—and then to have left it to the generations of the future to wage the inevitable war, unless, of course, our enemies recoiled when they found themselves faced with the newly acquired might of the German people. In this way, Germany would have been well equipped both materially and morally. She would have at her disposal an administration, a foreign policy and an army all moulded from infancy in the principles of National Socialism. The task I have undertaken of raising the German people to the place in the world that is their due is unfortunately not a task that can be accomplished by a single man or in a single generation. But I have at least opened their eyes to their inherent greatness and I have inspired them to exaltation at the thought of the union of Germans in one great indestructible Reich. I have sown the good seed. I have made the German people realize the significance of the struggle they are waging for their very existence.

One day the harvest will come, and nothing on earth will be able to prevent it from coming. The German people is a young and strong people, a people with its future before it.

XVI

Churchill's lack of appreciation—The irreparable could
have been avoided—Essentiality of forestalling Russian
attack—Italy prevents the opening of the campaign in
good time—Catastrophic consequences of the delay—
My illusion of a possible *entente* with Stalin

26th February 1945

In actual fact, my decision to settle the issue with Russia
by force of arms was taken as soon as I became convinced
that Britain was determined to remain stubborn. Churchill
was quite unable to appreciate the sporting spirit of which
I had given proof by refraining from creating an irreparable breach between the British and ourselves. We did,
indeed, refrain from annihilating them at Dunkirk. We
ought to have been able to make them realize that the
acceptance by them of the German hegemony established
in Europe, a state of affairs to the implementation of
which they had always been opposed, but which I had

implemented without any trouble, would bring them inestimable advantages.

Even by the end of July, one month, that is, after the defeat of France, I realized that peace was once again eluding our grasp. A few weeks later I knew that we should not succeed in invading Britain before the advent of the autumnal gales because we had not succeeded in acquiring complete command of the air. In other words, I realized that we should never succeed in invading Britain.

The attitude of the Russians during the summer of 1940, the fact that they had absorbed the Baltic States and Bessarabia while we ourselves were busy in the west left me with no illusions regarding their intentions. And even if I had retained any, Molotov's visit in November would have been sufficient to dissipate them. The proposals which Stalin submitted to me after the return of his Minister did not deceive me. Stalin, that incomparable and imperturbable blackmailer, was trying to gain time in order to consolidate his advanced bases in Finland and the Balkans. He was trying to play cat and mouse with us.

The tragedy, from my point of view, was the fact that I could not attack before 15th May, and if I were to succeed in my first initial onslaught, it was essential that I should not attack later than that date. Stalin, however, could have launched his attack much earlier. Throughout the winter of 1940, and even more so in the spring of 1941, I was haunted by the obsession that the Russians might take the offensive. In the event, the Italian defeats in Albania and in Cyrenaica had roused a minor storm of revolt in the Balkans. Indirectly, they also struck a blow at the belief in our invincibility, that was held by friend and foe alike.

This alone was the cause of Yugoslavia's *volte-face*, an event that compelled us to drag the Balkans into the war; and that was something which at all costs I had desired to avoid. For once we had become involved in that direction we might well have been tempted to go still further ahead. I need hardly say that in the spring of 1941 we could rapidly have liberated the Near East with only a small fraction of the forces which we were about to employ against Russia. But to have removed the necessary forces from their place in our order of battle at that juncture would have been to incur the indirect danger of giving Russia a signal to attack. They would have done so in the summer, or at the latest in the autumn, and under conditions so disastrous from our point of view, that we could never have hoped to win the day.

Where the Jew-ridden democracies are concerned, the Russians have the patience of an elephant. They know with absolute certainty that sooner or later and without recourse to war, they will succeed in establishing dominion over them, thanks to the internal dissensions that rend them, the succession of economic crises from which they seem unable to escape and the powerful lure of Marxism to which they are particularly vulnerable. But they also know that in the case of the Third Reich the situation is very different. They know that in every field of endeavour, and more so in peace than in war, we shall everywhere outclass them.

The explanation of this patience which the Russians exhibit is to be found in their philosophy, which allows them to avoid taking risks and to wait—a year, a generation, a century, if necessary—until the time is ripe for the implementation of their plans. Time means nothing to them. Marxism, certainly, has promised them a paradise on earth—but certainly not today, not even tomorrow, but some time in the dim, indefinite future.

Notwithstanding this patience which is the backbone of their power, the Russians could not stand idly aside and watch the destruction of Great Britain, for in that case, with the United States and Japan cancelling each other out, as it were, the Russians would find themselves face to face with us—and alone. And that would mean without any doubt that, at a time and a place of our choice, the long-outstanding issue between us would be settled in our favour.

If I felt compelled to decide to settle my accounts with Bolshevism by force of arms, and, indeed, arrived at my decision on the very anniversary of the signing of the Moscow pact, I have every right to believe that Stalin had come to the same decision even before he signed the pact.

For a whole year I adhered to the hope that an *entente*, at least honestly sincere if not unreservedly friendly, could be established between the Third Reich and Stalin's Russia. I imagined that after fifteen years of power Stalin, the realist, would have rid himself of the nebulous Marxist ideology and that he was preserving it merely as a poison reserved exclusively for external use. The brutal manner in which he decapitated the Jewish intelligentsia, who had rendered him such signal service in the destruction of Tsarist Russia, encouraged me in that belief. I presumed that he did not wish to give these same Jewish intellectuals the chance of bringing about the downfall of the totalitarian empire which he had built—that Stalinist empire which, in all its essentials, is only the spiritual successor to the empire of Peter the Great.

In a spirit of implacable realism on both sides we could have created a situation in which a durable *entente* would have been possible—by defining precisely the zones of influence to be attributed to each party, by rigorously restricting our collaboration to the field of economics and in such a manner that both parties would have derived benefits therefrom. An *entente*, in short, watched over by an eagle eye and with a finger on the trigger!

XVII

Europe's last chance—Napoleon and winning the peace
—Napoleon's agony and mine—Britain always bars our
way—Those who thrive on discord in Europe

26th February 1945

I have been Europe's last hope. She proved incapable of
refashioning herself by means of voluntary reform. She
showed herself impervious to charm and persuasion. To
take her I had to use violence.

Europe can be built only on a foundation of ruins.
Not material ruins, but on ruins of vested interests and
economic coalitions, of mental rigidity and perverse pre-
judice, of outmoded idiosyncrasy and narrow-mindedness.
Europe must be fashioned in the common interest of all
and without regard for individuals. Napoleon understood
that perfectly.

I, perhaps better than anyone else, can well imagine
the torments suffered by Napoleon, longing, as he was,

for the triumph of peace and yet compelled to continue waging war, without ceasing and without seeing any prospect of ceasing—and still persisting in the hope eternal of at last achieving peace. Since the summer of 1940 I have myself been suffering the same torments. And always it has been this Britain who barred Europe's way to prosperity. But now she is aged and enfeebled, though not less vicious and wicked. Finally, she is being supported in this negative and unnatural attitude by the United States, themselves inspired and urged on by the whole forces of international Jewry, which has flourished and hopes long to continue to flourish as the result of our dissensions.

XVIII

A defeat which must inevitably be complete—The
Reich hacked to pieces by the conquerors—A Germany
in transition—The resurrection of eternal Germany—
Lines of conduct for the faithful—The premier people
on the Continent—Britain and Italy, if only . . .—A
France degenerate and implacably hostile—Waiting for
the rise of the African and Asiatic peoples—The U.S.A.
and Russia face to face—A Russia rid of Marxism—The
frailty of the American colossus—The rights of fam-
ished peoples—The chances of survival for a courageous
people

2nd April 1945

If we are destined to be beaten in this war, our defeat will
be utter and complete. Our enemies have proclaimed their
objectives in a manner which leaves us no illusions as to
their intentions. Jews, Russian Bolshevists and the pack
of jackals that follows, yelping at their heels—we know
that none of them will lay aside their arms until they have
destroyed and annihilated National Socialist Germany and

reduced it to a heap of rubble. In a ghastly conflict like this, in a war in which two so completely irreconcilable ideologies confront one another, the issue can inevitably only be settled by the total destruction of one side or the other. It is a fight which must be waged, by both sides, until they are utterly exhausted; and for our part, we know that we shall fight on until victory is achieved or until our last drop of blood has been shed.

It is a cruel thought. It fills me with horror to think of our Reich hacked to pieces by the victors, our peoples exposed to the savage excesses of the Bolsheviks and the American gangsters. Even this prospect, however, does not shake my invincible faith in the future of the German people. The more we suffer, the more glorious will be the resurrection of eternal Germany! That characteristic of the German mind, to plunge into lethargy when it seems certain that the very existence of the nation is at stake, will once more stand us in good stead. But as far as I personally am concerned I could not bear to live in Germany during the transition period that would follow the defeat of the Third Reich. The ignominies and the treachery we experienced in 1918 will be as nothing in comparison with what we may now expect. It is beyond comprehension that, after twelve years of National Socialism, such a thing could happen. My imagination boggles at the idea of a Germany, henceforth deprived of her *élite* which led her to the very pinnacles of heroism, wallowing for years and years in the mire.

What advice can we give, then, what rules of conduct can we recommend to those who survive, with their souls untarnished and their hearts unshaken? Battered, left alone to work out its own salvation, existing solely as a custodian during the grim darkness of the night, the German people must strive its very utmost spontaneously to respect those racial laws which we laid down for it. In a world which is becoming more and more perverted through the Jewish virus, a people which has remained immune to the virus must in the long run emerge supreme. From this point of view, National Socialism can justly claim the eternal gratitude of the people for having eliminated the Jew from Germany and Central Europe.

Post-war Germany's second preoccupation should be to preserve indissoluble the union of all the German races. It is only when we are united that our qualities expand to their full stature; only when we cease to be Prussians, Bavarians, Austrians, Rhinelanders and become just Germans. The Prussians were the first to gather the Germans into one Reich under Bismarck, and by so doing gave the German people their opportunity to show that they were the premier people in Europe. I myself, by uniting them all in the Third Reich, set them on the path to become the architects of a new Europe. Whatever the future holds, the German peoples must remember that it is essential that they should cast out all elements that make for discord among them and should indefatigably pursue every measure which contributes to the maintenance of their unity.

As far as foreign countries are concerned, it is not possible to lay down rigid rules, for the situation is in a constant state of change. Twenty years ago, I wrote that there were only two possible allies in Europe for Germany —Britain and Italy. The course of events during this period has not been such as to permit the implementation of a policy which would have been the logical sequence to my statement. The British, admittedly, still wielded imperial power, but they no longer possessed the moral qualities requisite for the preservation of their empire. They seemed to dominate the world; in reality they were themselves dominated by the Jews. Italy had tried to emulate ancient Rome. She had all the Roman ambitions, but she lacked the two essential adjuncts of a determined spirit and material power. The only trump card she had was the leadership of a true Roman. What a tragedy for that man! And what a tragedy for that country! For a people, as for an individual, it is tragic to have ambitions and to lack both the means essential to their fulfilment and any hope of acquiring those means.

There remains France. Twenty years ago I wrote what I thought of France. She was and is the mortal enemy of the German people. Her steady degeneration and her frequent *crises de nerfs* have sometimes led us to minimize the importance of her actions. Should she continue to become more feeble, as seems probable, that will be no reason for us to become less distrustful of her. The military might of France is now nothing but a memory, and purely from that point of view you may be quite sure that she will never again cause us a moment's anxiety. Whatever may be the issue of it, this war has at least put France in the category to which she belongs—that of a fifth-class Power. Even so, thanks to her unlimited powers of corruption and her inimitable skill in the art of blackmail, she can still be a source of danger to us. Our watchwords therefore must be: mistrust and vigilance. Let the Germans take care never to allow themselves to be lulled by the voice of this syren!

While, therefore, it is not possible to adhere to rigid principles in dealing with foreign countries and one must always be prepared to adapt one's policy to the changing conditions, it can nevertheless be asserted with confidence that Germany will always recruit her staunchest friends from among those peoples who are actively resistant to Jewish contagion. I am sure that the Japanese, the Chinese and the peoples of Islam will always be closer to us than, for example, France, in spite of the fact that we are related by blood. It is a tragedy that France has consistently degenerated in the course of centuries and that her upper classes have been perverted by the Jews. France is now condemned to the pursuit of a Jewish policy.

With the defeat of the Reich and pending the emergence of the Asiatic, the African and, perhaps, the South American nationalisms, there will remain in the world only two Great Powers capable of confronting each other —the United States and Soviet Russia. The laws of both history and geography will compel these two Powers to a trial of strength, either military or in the fields of economics and ideology. These same laws make it inevitable that both Powers should become enemies of Europe. And it is equally certain that both these Powers will sooner or later find it desirable to seek the support of the sole surviving great nation in Europe, the German people. I say with all the emphasis at my command that the Germans must at all costs avoid playing the role of pawn in either camp.

At this juncture it is difficult to say which, from the ideological point of view, would prove to be the more injurious to us—Jew-ridden Americanism or Bolshevism. It is possible that under the pressure of events, the Russians will rid themselves completely of Jewish Marxism, only to re-incarnate pan-slavism in its most fierce and ferocious form. As for the Americans, if they do not swiftly succeed in casting off the yoke of New York Jewry (which has the same intelligence as a monkey that saws through the branch on which it is perching), well—it won't be long before they go under, before even having reached the age of maturity. The fact that they combine the possession of such vast material power with so vast a lack of intelligence evokes the image of some child stricken with elephantiasis. It may well be asked whether this is not simply a case of a mushroom civilization, destined to vanish as quickly as it sprang up.

If North America does not succeed in evolving a doctrine less puerile than the one which at present serves as a kind of moral *vade mecum* and which is based on lofty but chimerical principles and so-called Christian Science, it is questionable whether it will for long remain a predominantly white continent. It will soon become apparent that this giant with the feet of clay has, after its spectacular rise, just sufficient strength left to bring about its own downfall. And what a fine chance this sudden collapse will offer to the yellow races! From the point of view of both justice and history they will have exactly the same arguments (or lack of arguments) to support their invasion of the American continent as had the Europeans in the sixteenth century. Their vast and undernourished masses will confer on them the sole right that history recognizes—the right of starving people to assuage their hunger—provided always that their claim is well backed by force!

And so, in this cruel world into which two great wars have plunged us again, it is obvious that the only white peoples who have any chance of survival and prosperity are those who know how to suffer and who still retain the courage to fight, even when things are hopeless, to the death. And the only peoples who will have the right to claim these qualities will be those who have shown themselves capable of eradicating from their system the deadly poison of Jewry.

INDEX

Abetz, Otto, 60
Abyssinia, 72
Albania, 97
Algeria, 47, 61
Australia, 43, 46
Austria: Atticism of, 54; Anschluss, 74

Balkan States, 72–3, 85, 97–8
Baltic States, 97
Belgium, 35, 74
Benes, Edouard, 84
Berlin, 65
Bessarabia, 97
Bismarck, Prince von, 105
Bolshevism, Germany's essential task to destroy, 34, 66
Breslau, 78
Budapest, 78
Bulgaria, 66

Chamberlain, Neville, 80, 84
China, 107; pride of race, 53
Christianity, 44, 45; not a natural religion for Germans, 53–4; stronger than Marxism, 94
Churchill, Sir Winston, 72; compared with Pitt, 29–33; 'condemns his country to a policy of suicide', 30; 'Jew-ridden, half - American drunkard', 32, 33; his disappearance essential, 40; does not appreciate Hitler's sporting spirit, 96
Ciano, Count, 80–1

Colonization: exhausts a nation, 42–3; Germany and United States not interested in, 43, 46, 91; failure of European policy of, 45; French dislike of, 67
Cyrenaica, 72, 97
Czechoslovakia, 84–5

Delcassé, Théophile, 61
Dunkirk, 96

Egypt, 70, 71
Elizabeth Petrovna, Empress of Russia, 40
Europe: Pitt's policy in, 30; changes in balance of power, 30, 31, 32; unification of, prevented by Great Britain, 30, 32; failure of colonization policy, 45–6; Hitler her last hope, 101; United States and Russia inevitable enemies of, 107

Ferry, Jules, 67
Finland, 66, 97
France: defeat of, 33, 35, 70, 74, 78, 97; exhausted by colonial enterprises, 43; mistaken collaboration with, 60–2; 'a raddled old strumpet', 60; Germany should have liberated colonies of, 61; mortal enemy of Germany, 62, 106–7; and

III